SACRED DWELLING

SACRED DWELLING

A Spirituality of Family Life

WENDY M. WRIGHT

CROSSROAD · NEW YORK

1990
The Crossroad Publishing Company
370 Lexington Avenue, New York, N.Y. 10017

Library of Congress Cataloging-in-Publication Data

Wright, Wendy M.
  Sacred dwelling : a spirituality of family life / Wendy M. Wright.
    p. cm.
  Bibliography : p.
  ISBN 0-8245-0972-2
  1. Family—Religious life.   2. Spirituality.   I. Title.
BV4526.2.W75   1989
249—dc20   89-33049
                                                     CIP

For
Roger, Emily, Elizabeth, and Charles
with whom I dwell
in sacred space

Contents

Preface: Turning Home   9
Acknowledgments   15

APPROACH TO THE HOME   17

WITHIN   27

1. A Matter of the Heart   29
2. A Time for Wonder   41
3. The Christ-Room   52
4. Body of Christ   61
5. A Way That You Know Not   69

DEEPER WITHIN   81

6. Male and Female God Created Them   83
7. In the Circle of a Mother's Arms   101
8. Wreathed in Flesh and Warm   113
9. Transfiguration   125
10. A Vowed Life   136

LOOKING OUT   153

11. Circles of Care   155
12. A Place of Springs   170
13. The *Is-ness* of Things   187

Notes   199

Preface
Turning Home

'Tis the gift to be simple
'Tis the gift to be free
'Tis the gift to come down where we ought to be
And when we find ourselves in a place just right
'Twill be in the valley of love and delight.

When true simplicity is gained
To bow and to bend we shan't be ashamed
To turn, turn, 'twill be our delight
'Til by turning, turning we come round right.

Traditional Shaker tune

This book has grown out of my personal struggle to integrate the two most significant facets of my life: my family and my Christian spiritual heritage. One might not necessarily think that integration should be needed between the two realms of experience that are so audible in contemporary Christian rhetoric. But my discovery has been that, if one pushes the rhetoric beyond surface meaning, the need for integration really does exist. This need is not particular to me but is shared by the wider Church as well.

While pursuing my doctoral studies in the history of Christian spirituality, I had the opportunity to delve into a storehouse of treasures. I fell in love with the great mystics and ascetics of our Church's past, those who witnessed with such passionate integrity to the gospel's power to unleash the deepest human potential and recreate human community through the Spirit of God. I experienced the capacity of prayer and silence to reshape the human heart and saw in our contemplative tradition a vision of reality that challenged and invited me.

But I also learned that our tradition contained some assumptions about the mode of living required to cultivate an authentic spiritual life that excluded Christians living the ordinary life. While our recorded spiritual teaching contains much wisdom that can nourish Christians in all walks of life, some is limited by the authors' experience. Much of the classic literature was created by persons, the majority of them men, who lived as celibates in monastic community, as hermits, as mendicant preachers, or as apostolic religious. These writers assumed, with the sanction of religious and cultural authority, that their way of life (ascetic, celibate, usually monastic) was especially spiritual because it was conducive to the cultivation of the disciplines long associated with prayer and because it approached the state of being that God intended for humankind.

However, I was married and soon began to have children. For all the love I held for the tradition's treasures, there were few words about what I began to experience as the most intimate and God-centered dynamics of my life. Instead, the literature either ignored my lived experience or positively disdained it as a context within which one could achieve spiritual maturity. This came home to me one day as I was reading a treatise by St. Jerome, a fourth-century champion of the monastic life and one of the most influential of the church fathers. In it he articulated the assumptions of our spiritual heritage with vivid clarity.

> She that is unmarried is careful for the things of the Lord that she may be holy both in body and spirit; but she that is married is careful of the things of the world, how she may please her husband. . . . Do you think there is no difference between one who spends her time in prayer and fasting and one who must, at her husband's approach, make up her countenance, walk with mincing gait and feign a show of endearment? . . . Then come the prattling of infants, the noisy household, children

waiting for her word and waiting for her kiss, the reckoning up of expenses, the preparation to meet the outlay. . . . The wife flies like a swallow all over the house. She has seen to everything. Is the sofa smooth? Is dinner ready? Tell me, pray, where amid all this is there room for the thought of God?[1]

Jerome's flamboyant style aside, the assumptions about the intrinsically more spiritual nature of celibacy as compared with marriage and family life that his words betray persisted in Catholic circles up into this century and linger still in disguised forms. While the Protestant churches have, from their inceptions, reversed the positions of marriage and celibacy in the rank order of spiritual goods, Protestants also have tended to lose the thread connecting them to the classic literature of prayer.

So the need I discovered—to integrate family and traditional spirituality—was both my own and that of the wider Christian community. This effort at integration, which I think is the task of Christian families aided by the gathered Church, is fairly strenuous. On the one hand, this involves a return to our past to look again with loving eyes at our spiritual treasures so that we can draw from them what speaks authentically to us, and, on the other hand, to reclaim or reunderstand the essential religious truth of what does not immediately hold meaning for us.

The bold activity of naming for ourselves the sacred times, places, and people that we encounter in our families is also necessary. For this we need to affirm the intrinsically sacramental quality of all life. We need new eyes to see into the often opaque fabric of our ordinary routine and to discern there the depth dimension, the call of Christ, the face of God.

Our search for integration calls us to articulate a way of being Christian that is in continuity with our rich heritage but not limited to it. To do this we may need to re-image the most basic metaphors that now carry for us the connotations of God and spirituality. For instance, Christians are familiar with the image of the spiritual life as a journey or pilgrimage or battle. Our tradition gives us a wonderful literature that develops these metaphors and teaches us that the spiritual life is a process of overcoming and of going from "here" to "there." The quest for the Grail, the battles of warfare with demons in the desert, the "way" of the itinerant pilgrim, all speak to us of this.

These metaphors spring not only from foundational patterns that motivate the human psyche but also from the patterns of living and experience of those who live in solitude or outside the confines of the radical intimacy one finds in family. It reflects the experience of those who are not bound by the particular cares and responsibilities of family and who may literally journey into the wilderness.

What we lack as a Christian community is a language for the spiritual life that also speaks in terms of settled habitation. We need the freedom to imagine ourselves not only as "journeying" but also as "dwelling." We need to see that we need not always enter new landscapes in order to grow in God, that we can also cultivate a settled space and make it richer and more inhabited with meaning. We do this in much the same way that we come to experience a home that over time holds within its walls a store of multilayered and telling memories communicating a wealth of insight.[2] We need to "turn" home.

This turning has several dimensions. We can "turn" in the same sense of being converted. "Turn to me and be saved, says the Lord!" To turn as an act of religious conversion implies a return, a coming home again to God, our origin and end. It also suggests the turning inside out that our hearts must experience for us to turn round "right." We must set our love and our hopes on the deepest level of our lives. Turning around also evokes a sense of seeing anew, of seeing into what was always there in a new way. This is what we mean when we say, "I really had my thinking turned around."

Further, we familied people who inhabit homes, who live among and with people who give us identity, whom we serve, by whom we are served, need to turn to our experience. We need to reflect on our homes and intimate relationships. We need to turn them around just as we would turn over and admire a handcrafted piece of pottery that has been given us to appreciate.

So the purpose of *Sacred Dwelling* is twofold. First, it suggests a thoroughly Christian spirituality that is derived from the experience of living in family and that is in continuity with our spiritual heritage. Second, this book explores the dynamics of such a family spirituality in terms that are spatial and in metaphors that suggest the spiritual richness of the processes of dwelling: homemaking, intimacy, gestating, nurturing, remembering, cultivating, harvesting.

Sacred Dwelling is structured as a contemplative walk through a home, allowing the various rooms, pieces of furniture, and objects to evoke a sense of the lived experience of inhabiting and being in family. In this walk we will come upon the ways in which family members sense the presence of the indwelling God and the ways in which they respond to the passionate call of God truly to become transfigured people.

Acknowledgments

There is a larger family beyond my own whose influence is felt in the pages of this book. Without them, it could not have been conceived or written. They are due many thanks. First, Marie Cantlon has been involved, as editor, from the book's inception. Her whittling down of my sometimes baroque prose has given these paragraphs a lean elegance. Mickey McGrath, O.S.F.S., has given my thoughts graceful visual expression in his cover drawing. Jackie Lynch of Omaha put the manuscript, in its many phases, onto the word processor and Doug Lee-Regier nurtured my pre-schoolers while I was busy writing. To both of them special thanks are due.

Richard Clifford, S.J., past dean of Weston School of Theology in Cambridge, and Claudia Blanchette, S.N.D., director of the Institute of Educational and Pastoral Ministry at Emmanuel College in Boston possessed the imagination to allow me to develop a new course in family spirituality at their respective institutions. Barb Markey, N.D., of the Office of Family Life in Omaha, was generous in the support that made the writing of *Sacred Dwelling* possible. John Mogabgab and the staff of *Weavings* have been, over the last several years, a source of encouragement and inspiration. Two of the essays found here, "In the Circle of a Mother's Arms" and "Wreathed in Flesh and Warm" previously appeared in *Weavings* (vol. 3, no. 1 and vol. 2, no. 1). Permission to reprint a segment of "Where Our Roots Are" was granted by Charles Fenyvesi and *Organic Gardening*.

Finally, the students in my courses at Emmanuel and Weston and the participants in workshops on family spirituality that I

15

have given in any number of places are present in these pages. Some of their stories are here; many of their questions and insights are reflected also. Their sharing of what is most sacred to them has expanded my own personal story immeasurably and made it, I hope, a story that we all can share.

APPROACH TO THE HOME

Will you, God, really live with people on earth?
Why, the heavens and their own heavens cannot
    contain you.
How much less this house that I have built. . . .
    Listen to the cry and to the prayer I make
    to you today.
Day and night let your eyes watch over this
    house, over this place of which you have
    said "My name shall be there."

1 Kings 8:27–29

I do not intend to describe for you in minute detail the appearance of the home. That is for you to do. Nor will I paint a portrait of the family that lives inside. They are yours to identify. What I hope is that through a process of association and imagination you will find your own home and family here. I will suggest that, according to sociological and demographic studies of the American family, you will describe the homes and families that are yours in a diversity of ways.[1] Only a small percentage of you will be able to construct an accurate picture of your life-situation by appealing to what I might call the myth of the American family: a working father (smiling), a stay-at-home mother (smiling), two children (smiling), perhaps a dog, a single-family dwelling surrounded by a neat lawn.

Many of you may be tempted to call up this culturally treasured image when the word *family* is mentioned. But most of you

19

will not be able to find yourselves reflected there. Instead, your family will fit a variety of configurations: divorced or separated, widowed, single-parent, stepparent, childless, blended, adoptive, multigenerational, aging. Your homes will be equally diverse in appearance. You will live in high rises, apartment complexes, condominiums, farmhouses, tenement buildings, trailer courts, duplexes, hotels, rented rooms or in community with other families. Most of you will have moved many times. Most of you are more familiar with city streets than manicured lawns bordering your homes.

Very few of you are smiling all the time. Most of your families are scarred to one degree or another by death, disease, alcoholism, drug addiction, violence, spouse-battering, child abuse, lack of communication, quarreling between generations, quarreling with in-laws. Most of you find the fabric of your relationships stretched unbearably by the pull of contemporary life. You are stamped with the violence and jaundiced view of human society that is reflected in the media. You are oppressed by the pressures of succeeding or of simply getting by, overwhelmed with financial worry, seduced by a consumerist view of ultimate happiness, absent from one another's lives because of the sheer number of commitments forced on you by jobs, schools, peer and collegial pressure, duty, or the desire for some sort of personal enhancement.[2]

Despite all this, most of you will also look to your home and family as a primary source of nurture and meaning. You will accept the idea that home in some way represents (or should represent) a foundational experience of caring community. I think this is not just an unfounded and culturally induced illusion.[3] Both philosophically and psychologically the concept of home has been explored as a powerful and primal image in which our deepest being is rooted. The home has been held to be an essential image in the phenomenology of the imagination, a concentration of the entire psyche, our first universe.[4] Child psychologists, when they want to ascertain the self-image of a young client, will often ask the girl or boy to draw a picture of a house. The home as an image can reflect a sense of identity and meaning-making that contains within itself a clue to the way we understand ourselves and our world.

The term home has religious associations for us as well. In most faiths home connotes a place of ultimate rest and comfort, of belonging and identity, of being with God. This is remarkably true of our Judeo-Christian legacy. To be reminded of this, one need only recall the Psalms with their frequent references to Yahweh's dwelling place or bring to mind the poignant melody of the traditional American hymn from which the words so easily flow:

> Softly and tenderly,
> Jesus is calling
> Calling to carry me home.
> Come home, come home.

So for us calling up the concept of home evokes several clusters of ideas and brings into play a spectrum of associative meanings that operate on many levels of our self-awareness. We experience home as representing the American myth which in turn gives expression to our collective longings for a stable and caring environment and community. We also experience home on the level of religious consciousness as answering our hearts' cries for meaning and ultimacy—"home" is also "homecoming."

At the same time that we usher in these almost archetypal images of home, we also recognize the current reality of our own homes and families. There may be considerable disjuncture between these sets of data. But this gap need not be uncreative. Nor, I think, should we be deterred from looking at our unidealized life situations as potential windows through which to touch and be touched by God's presence. While our "real" homes may not always conform to our "ideal" homes, there is a profound relationship between the two.

By this I do not mean to suggest that we imagine ourselves as other than we are. This is not a book that will attempt to articulate a spirituality exclusively out of the experience of the "perfect" or even the clinically "functional" family.[5] After all, an authentic spiritual life assumes that we start exactly where we are, not in some unattained ideal realm. God cannot find us in any place other than the one in which we find ourselves. But neither is this a book that ignores the profound spiritual yearning in each of us to "come home," to realize the "more," both the "more" of what we would want our families to be and the desire for "more" that spurs our religious seeking.

Within this lived tension our spiritual lives are cultivated: the tension between the factuality of our daily lives with their monotony, opaqueness, limitations, and sorrows with occasional moments of insight and beauty, and the equally factual but less realized soarings of our hearts. "Home" for each of us is at the lived center of this creative tension.

The Roof and Foundation of the Christian Home

Therefore the "home" into which you are about to enter is not a generic family dwelling, but rather a unique constellation of persons gathering together (permanently, temporarily, or occasionally) within the shelter of a variety of structures that house and express that unique network of interrelationships.

Yet in all this diversity there is also a unity to these homes that harkens back to their archetypal aspect. They all share in the perception that there is a "more" about our lives that calls out for articulation and asks for a response. In Christian homes, whatever their denomination, this "more" is in part connected to the idea that God is now truly present to us, woven into the fabric of our lives, present and waiting to be perceived and celebrated. This is what might be termed the *mystical* dimension of Christian life.

In many ways this mystical dimension is the foundation of spirituality in the home. This intuition, dug from and constructed in the stuff of creation itself, is that God's own life can somehow be touched here and now, in the faces, places, and events of our ordinary daily rounds. This is an intuition that arises, I think, from the core of the created world and from humankind's most rooted self-knowledge. We as Christians celebrate this intuition at Christmastime: God is with us, God is born among us, Deity becomes enfleshed in blood and bone, the immensity of divine life is gestated in the human womb.

While this mystical dimension is the foundation of the family's spiritual life, there is another profound human intimation that is common to our diversity of homes. This is that the "more" we sense we are called to is not only discovered to be hidden in whatever is—the "more" is also an arresting call to become other than what we are at present. This apprehension I would term the *prophetic* dimension of the Christian family and I would liken it to the roof of the home. The prophetic call is the highest upward thrusting element of the entire structure, the architectural feature of the house that most obviously speaks of the aspiration that lives within.

Most Christian families live between the tension of "already but not yet";[6] God is indeed with us but not yet in fullness. And something is required of us, some seeking, some response, some radical restructuring that enables us to become more the way God would have us. The family, as well as the individual, must experience this prophetic dimension of life to be authentically Christian. While the prophetic perspective is deeply embedded in all facets of our faith, Passiontide and Easter are when we celebrate its fullest expanse. Then we proclaim that humankind's dearest hopes are fulfilled, that God does not simply enter into the substance of history but that God transfigures history utterly. We allow our hopes and our imaginations to soar beyond what we humanly perceive to the limitless expanse of divine love. We look beyond death to life risen, triumphant and full.

The spiritual life of the Christian family comes into being between this roof and this foundation, between the prophetic and mystical dimensions of our faith. As we grow in our apprehension of what God calls us to, we struggle to awaken to the sacred quality of what we are and to respond to the challenge of what we might be.

The Family as Domestic Church

In this the family is not greatly different from any other part of the Christian community. The faithful, after all, *are* the Church. My impression, however, is that families do not often think of themselves as church. At best, families either simply claim agreement with official church doctrine or import "churchy" rituals or prayers into their homes hoping this will impart religious meaning to their shared life. Most Christian families seem not to feel their very family-ness as sacred. They fail to name their most profound moments of shared memory—birth, death, sexual intimacy, estrangement, forgiveness, gathering, the daily struggles to be with and for each other—with words associated with religion or the spiritual life. Yet, in the documents that came out of the Second Vatican Council in the 1960s, the Roman Catholic tradition did explicitly name the family as "domestic church" (a phrase first coined by St. Jerome!).[7] While the full implications of introducing these words into the vocabulary of accepted discourse may not have been envisioned by those who spoke them, nevertheless, their existence is significant and their intrinsic meaning is being drawn out now by those who live the experience of domestic church.[8]

That the Christian family is understood to be an authentic, and indeed, the primary unit of church does not necessarily mean that the family mirrors in miniature the institutional church in its structure or simply that family members embrace official teaching. Nor does it mainly mean that "religion starts at home" (although this is undoubtedly often the case).

Rather to be the domestic church means that the family, in the uniqueness of its way-of-being-in-the-world (as an intimate physical, psychological, and spiritual entity) is an authentic community of believers. What the members of the family know to be their own experience of the sacred in the particularities of marriage, sexual intimacy, procreation, parenting; the building, sustaining and decay of intimate relationships; the struggles of providing, sheltering, and feeding—this experience is authentic and must be part of the knowledge of the gathered church. The ways that the family senses a call to witness to the gospel are true vocations and serve the whole. The family as authentic church can, and must, inform the whole Church of the ways it touches God and of the vocations that it provides. In other words, church teaching and Christian witness must come directly, at least in part, from the lived experience of family.

This way of viewing family as domestic church could have profound consequences for the larger gathered Church if the wider body truly began to learn from families what it means to be Christian community. Perhaps church as "the professionals doing for the nonprofessionals" or church as "committees that direct programs," or church as "fix-it shop for crises" or church as "social club" might give way to a renewed vision of Christian community.

The family, for its part, must learn to trust the fact that it is a living and authoritative cell of the Church. It must know itself to be a community of persons tenderly fashioned by a loving creative hand, a community that tries to respond to that love by listening to the word that God speaks in Scripture, tradition, the experience of being together and through the person of Jesus Christ, a community that, by hearing, becomes the word of God spoken anew. The family needs to know itself as a people deeply blessed and deeply broken, a people who must celebrate the gift of life itself and the gift that is each individual life. The family is called to care for and empower each of its members, not simply for the sake of individual self-actualization, but also for the sake of the whole Church and all of God's creation.

The family shares this mission with the gathered Church. But the family's ways of being church are distinctive. Its ways have only partly to do with the ways the Christian community has chiefly identified itself as Church in the past: seeking God in the desert, in silence and solitude, in celibacy, in the freedom of detachment or of voluntary poverty, and in the consciousness of the transitoriness of human life. The family's ways of being Church have as much to do with inhabiting, with the co-penetration of bodies and hearts, with the dense fabric of human attachments, with busyness and business, with the labors of providing, with touching and being touched, with consciousness of the continuity and permanency of human existence. The domestic church enfleshes the Word of God in a distinctive way that must enrich the self-understanding of the entire Church.

Between the foundation and the roof of the Christian home, in the lived tension between the mystical and prophetic calls, church community comes alive. No two domestic churches are identical, but they all share in the intimacy of incarnate divinity and so present to the entire Church and to the world the human face and vital activity of God's own life.

WITHIN

·1·

To enter the door of a home is to pass through a structure that evokes what anthropologists term a *liminal state*, a transitional passage between two phases in the life cycle. A liminal state is a time of ritual power and danger between an old phase which is passing away and a new phase that has not yet come into being. It is a time to be ritually celebrated. The doorway of the home is an architectural expression of the continuous liminality that characterizes the life of the family gathered within.

This is the passageway through which a groom carries his bride, a new child may be brought, under which daily kisses of leave-taking and return are exchanged, through which a new college student embarks on a journey of self-discovery, or through which a grandparent leaves for the last time. At the doorway we mark the transitions. We recognize that life is most full and complete when all the family's members are together within the home. But we also recognize that, in fact, this rarely occurs.

The doorway expresses the liminality of the rhythmic gathering and dispersal that is part of family experience. The door is the narrow passage through which the family enters to reunite and through which the family passes when its wholeness fragments into discrete parts. The doorway is thus a sacred space of welcome and leave-taking.

A Matter of the Heart

> I will give them a new heart and a new spirit. I will take
> the heart of stone from their bodies and give them a heart
> of flesh instead. . . . then they shall be my people and I will
> be their God.
>
> Ezekiel 11:17–20

I sit on the edge of my son's bed. His face is smooth with sleep.
The glow of the nightlight stands vigil against the "monsters"
that he worries lurk beneath his changing table. In the warm
dark of the room, the two rhythms of our breathing punctuate
the silence. As I stand up to leave, I feel my heart, utterly self-
contained a moment before, nearly pulled from my breast,
stretched to span the widening distance between us. A presence,
palpable in its intensity, connects us. Before he was born, I did
not know how I could ever let him in. Now that I have, I don't
know how I will ever let him go.

Becoming family is many things. It involves, in part, the acceptance of adult responsibility, nurturing and guiding the helpless
and unformed, and passing on the living fund of culture, knowledge, and wisdom from one generation to the next. But being
family as a spiritual discipline is, I think, a matter of the heart.
And that involves the reformation of the core of our beings, a
radical expanding of the established contours of our hearts to include others in a permanent and life-altering way.

Any genuine experience of love alters the heart and creates it
anew. It gentles us. For authentic love is not a transient emotion

30

but a spiritual dynamic of immense power that we as Christians know to be stronger than anything else, even death. To love at the deepest level of our beings is to participate in the birth of our God who is love. This is not a simple matter. Family life is an especially demanding discipline of loving because, in a heightened way, it calls for an increased capacity of the heart to love a person as totally other and to love them enough to let them go. The great and twin disciplines of the spiritual art of being family are, I think, the disciplines of welcoming and of letting go. These are matters of the heart.

Welcoming

Our son was baptized by immersion at the 10:00 A.M. Sunday liturgy at our parish in Boston. The sacrament was enacted to impress upon all of us present the full import of this ritual of welcome that was taking place. After the reading of the Word my husband and I, our two daughters, and the designated godparents came forward before the entire gathered community to celebrate the entry of this new Christian into our midst.

Our associate pastor, a talented liturgist, presided wonderfully over the event. Called to consciousness of our own baptismal promises, sprinkled with the cleansing waters that flew from the tips of a fragrant green bough, we proceeded to undress our tiny infant and offer him, naked and squealing, to the waters of the baptismal font. Then we robed him in the white garments of his new life. We—parents, godparents and congregation—vowed to accept the responsibility for welcoming this child, for instructing him in the ways of faith and for being for him the Church, the body of Christ. He was welcomed home.

Several weeks later we were present at the same morning liturgy, this time seated among the congregation in the right apse of the church. Again our associate pastor presided. That morning there were several small children present in the assembly (our church had no "crying room"). None of the children were exceptionally unruly, but all of them were fidgety. The gospel was a striking one and when our celebrant mounted the pulpit, it was clear from his demeanor that he had planned (as he sometimes did) a special and dramatic homily to explicate the verses just read. As he began in hushed tones, the children opposite us dropped something. Our startled son, who was nestled on my lap, let out a wail. I attempted to soothe him but it became clear that what he really wanted was to nurse, so I tried to get him situated so that he would quiet down. Suddenly I became aware that there was silence from the pulpit. "Some of you may not be happy with this," the celebrant announced, "but I would really rather not be interrupted just now." I felt my face turn hot and tried to shush the baby, but I was so flustered nothing would do. So I picked him up and headed for the back of the church. Our presider waited to continue while I walked the length of the side aisle and exited out the doors. (I later learned that the family opposite also escaped the church at the first moment possible.)

I found myself standing in the sunshine confused and shocked. Moments later my husband emerged. "Well, if they're going to throw you out, I'm not going to stay," he announced. I couldn't imagine going back in, but our car was blocked in the parking lot so there was nothing to do but wait miserably until mass was over. During the wait I realized I was not only embarrassed, I was angry. Angry that it should be assumed that we were not trying our best to maintain a proper spirit of reverence. Angry that that church, which so recently was the gathering of a spirited community, now should be more like a concert performance with strict rules of decorum. Most of all I was angry that the whole notion of welcoming was so little understood in our church. And I did not mean just our local parish but our whole Church.

Any parent knows what it means to welcome a child. The entry of new life does not call for a polite if celebrative ritual and then a return to business as usual. Nor does it mean that you just schedule this person into your established routine like an appointment or meeting. You don't make a little space in your day or share a little concern and then wish the infant Godspeed. To welcome a child is to accept responsibility for another person twenty-four hours a day, seven days a week, for a good many years and, ultimately, to welcome the unfolding mystery of an entire lifetime's joys and pains as your own. To welcome a child is to give priority to the unpredictability of another life, to tend it in sickness, no matter what you had otherwise planned, to allow your plans and dreams to be altered, even set aside, because of another's need. To welcome a child is to learn to think and speak in response to a different and constantly changing worldview, to be outside of your own frame of reference. You learn patience and judgment and are confronted with your own very real and heretofore untested limitations. To welcome a child is to recognize the surprising expansiveness of your own capacity to love and to confront the shattering truth of your own violence and self-centeredness.

To welcome a child is to have your heart stretched, made capable of loving in a new and unrepeatable way. My sense is that this occurrence is very much a part of spiritual maturity, of being reformed into a closer likeness to the God by whom we are all created. One of the central tenents of our Christian faith is that we are made in the image and likeness of Deity itself. Only we are not mirror images. By human choice (the Fall), the image of God in us is diminished or (in the thinking of some Christians) virtually effaced. The central dynamic of each of our individual and collective lives must be to restore or receive again that lost image and likeness, to find our true identity. (Again, depending on which ends of the denominational spectrum you stand, you as individual may be presumed to have more or less responsibility for this process of restoration.) The Roman Catholic position is that the image of God is "wounded" or "tarnished" and that we, with God's grace and our own efforts can begin to "heal" or "cleanse" the lost image.

Our hearts are central in this process, for they must be made to resemble the heart of the one human being who perfectly embod-

ied in himself the life of God. Our hearts must become like the
heart of Jesus. In the classic literature of Christian spirituality, the
activity of this reformation comes under the rubric of "con-
quering the vices and acquiring the virtues." Certain inner dispo-
sitions—the virtues—are seen to be the qualities of person that
Jesus exemplified. In fact, in some of the literature they are
thought to be gifts of the Spirit of Jesus. The traditional list of
virtues includes faith, hope, charity, prudence, temperance, forti-
tude, and justice. Alongside these the church community has accepted as normative certain qualities of character suggested in
Jesus' teaching. Chief among these are the Beatitudes which represent not simply an otherworldly prophecy of reward and justice
for those who suffer on earth, but articulate the very qualities of
person from which blessing comes. Among the Beatitudes purity,
or singleness of heart, has for some time arrested my attention.

Not too long ago, during an Ignatian retreat, I had the opportunity to spend a considerable amount of reflective time with the
Beatitudes. Purity of heart, I found, was something I understood
only intellectually. Yes, I was sure that one of the major ways this
beatitude was interpreted in our spiritual heritage was as a sort
of single-focused quality of heart. One loved God alone. Or one
loved others primarily as an outflowing of the love that one had
for God. Purity of heart was associated, in the tradition, with the
virtue of detachment. In the fine commentary I was reading during the retreat, purity of heart was described with reference to the
biblical narratives about the calling of the disciples. Jesus' followers were described as exemplary because when they were called
they dropped their nets immediately and did not look back. In the
purity of their hearts the disciples gave precedence to the one call
they felt precluded any other concern.

As I tried to focus imaginatively on these scenes of discipleship
and to put myself into their frame of reference, I had the uneasy
feeling that something was not included here. I kept seeing the
wives and children of these impetuous men standing at the doors
of their fisherman's huts watching husbands and fathers drop

their nets and start off without a backward glance. These men's perfect purity of heart was, in fact, an utter detachment from the ordinary concerns of everyday life and relationships. I was not convinced.

I certainly did not want to imagine the men refusing to follow Jesus because they had families and jobs, but my meditation wouldn't allow the scenario to be played out in the traditional "detachment" interpretation. So I decided to imagine how the *women* who followed Jesus might have responded to his invitation. (It seemed a fair experiment since no one has bothered to record the stories of *their* calls for us.) Yes, the women heard the radical nature of the call. Yes, they knew that in fact Jesus' message was the one essential message that must be heard so that all else (home, family, work, etc.) could have real meaning.

But they did not drop all and walk away. Instead, the women returned to their families with the face and voice of Jesus burning in their hearts. They returned, knowing that the tender love they bore their children, spouses, parents, and friends, could never be effaced. But this new and powerful love was forcing its way into their hearts alongside and even beneath the other loves. They spoke to their families about the desire to follow this strange man. The women arranged for all their dependents to be taken care of or, where the parting would be too searing, they would carry their small children with them. And then they followed, hearts full, almost torn with the depth and richness of the loves they carried away with them (and to which they hoped to return with new zest). The entry of love into these women's hearts had reshaped and enlarged their very capacity for it.

No. This beatitude, in the only way that I could grasp it, did not mean the kind of singleness or purity of heart that is narrow or excludes other loves but rather an expansiveness of heart that gathers in all the loves and then orders them, not in rank order, one "better" than the others, but as if the deepest and most sustaining love was the love of God to which Jesus called the women. Then all other loves were made transparent by that love.

Through those particular loves of friend, husband, parent, child, the vast and nurturing love of God could be seen. Yes, this was the meaning of that beatitude for the women who followed Jesus.

To welcome a child, to welcome any family member, is to love this way. With each addition, the heart opens a little more. The heart acquires a capacity to love a little differently, to respond in compassion to a new personality, to willingly participate in the drama of an unfolding life. The spiritual discipline of family life, I think, is to allow this re-creation of the heart to take place. It also involves allowing the love you have for those with whom you are intimate to become transparent enough that the love of God can be seen through it.

Letting Go

"Attachment" is a word that has something of a negative connotation in the history of Christian spirituality. Anything to which a follower of Jesus is inordinately attached tends to be seen as a distraction from, or an obstruction to, the pure love of God and a hindrance to a ministry that is free to respond radically to the call to come and follow. St. Ignatius of Loyola's instructions at the beginning of his *Spiritual Exercises* are illustrative of this approach.

> We call spiritual exercises every way of preparing and disposing the soul to rid itself of all inordinate attachments, and after their removal, of seeking and finding the will of God in the disposition of our life for the salvation of our soul.[1]

I do not mean to obscure the subtlety and maturity with which the virtue of detachment has been expounded and lived in our tradition. But for many committed Christians detachment has meant, first of all, a refusal to attach deeply to any particular person (or ministry or idea for that matter). Celibacy makes perfect sense in this context. And while there are more persuasive and positive reasons for the embrace of celibacy set forth in today's literature, the fact remains that our tradition has for the most part de-emphasized and even discredited the arts of attachment and human intimacy.[2]

Certainly, being inordinately attached to a family member because of the esteem or profit you think they will bring you or because they are living out your unattained fantasies, is destructive. In terms of children, there cannot be any genuine parenting without first having a real and unalterable experience of bonding with a child. The deep attachment to the child is nurtured and grows over the course of many years. The bonding does not go away even if the child leaves or dies. For when our hearts have been stretched to make a special place for that unique love, they do not shrink again when the loved one has left the nest or been taken away by the violence of death. The heart always remains molded by the shape of that love.

Still it is true that the twin disciplines of family are welcoming *and* letting go. Letting go does not consist of ceasing to love, or detaching oneself from the affection one feels, but in loving more. Letting go involves radical faith. It means entrusting what you most love to the expansive care and protection of God. By this I do not mean that if you pray hard enough, God will not keep all the awful things that could happen, from happening to your child. Nor that every evil, even evil perpetrated on the innocent, is somehow "all in God's plan." But that somehow God's presence is available to us even in the mysteries of human suffering and death. Our trust is in a God whose presence accompanies us in every facet of human experience, a God who celebrates, laughs, plays, weeps, wonders, and is seared with pain just as we are. This kind of radical trust in an accompanying God is what allows us to let go. We let go not only so that our children can become independent adults guiding their own lives, but also so that God as Father and as Mother may parent them and we all may know ourselves as children of God.

Two images, both of snow, come to me in relation to the spiritual discipline of letting go. The first is of a day, not too long ago, when I was leading a retreat in rural Nebraska for a group of high school juniors from a Catholic boys' school. It was January and, though the day was clear, a stiff, frigid snow covered the ground. Late the previous night we had received a phone call from my eighty-three-year-old mother-in-law who was to undergo emergency surgery the next day. My husband hurriedly canceled appointments and set out early in the morning to be with her. Both of us were afraid, because of the gravity of the reports, that this might be the last time he would see her. Our letting go of her, and her of us, was very much on my mind as I entered the retreat.

I had never conducted an all-boy retreat before and had only recently begun doing this kind of work with high-school-age retreatants. They were a delightful group of young men on the verge of adulthood, filled with plans for the future: college, career, marriage. Each individual story took on life as the day progressed. I thought of my own son, still so little. What would he be like at sixteen? What school would he be going to? College, career, marriage? I was filled with his yet to be explored future.

During the afternoon break, I took a solitary walk on the grounds of the retreat center. Trees were bare, the air still and cold. The sharp sound of frozen snow giving way under my feet punctuated the silence. I climbed the crest of a hill and found myself in an old graveyard. My heart followed my husband who was driving south to be with his mother as she went into surgery. The dead, whose lives had been played out a century ago, were encased in small mounds of snow that splintered beneath my feet. At the far side of the graveyard a low tombstone caught my eye. Carved on its uppermost curve was an infant lamb worn smooth by the passage of nearly one hundred winters. The gravestone was that of two children, a little girl and a little boy, just the ages of my youngest daughter and son. They had died one day apart. No doubt an illness carried them off. How had their parents met the sudden loss? How deep was their trust in the God who alone would hold this little girl and boy from then on? And my trust? Could it be so tested?

We all were together for a silent moment on this snow-crusted hill: those long-ago children whose futures had been clipped off so abruptly; my own children whose futures, in my mind at least, stretched into an open-ended expanse of years; the young retreatants and their parents letting them go to face the coming years; my husband and his mother journeying both closer and farther away from each other; the dead beneath my living feet. We were together, our hearts made more pliant, gentle, tender, by allowing ourselves to love enough to let go.

The second snowy image is of a February day in Cambridge several years ago. Friends of ours, he a graduate student at Harvard Divinity School, had been expecting their fourth child just after we had given birth to our third. Their child, a boy, was born somewhat prematurely. For the first half-day, he seemed in excellent condition. His mother cradled and nursed him. His brothers and sisters came to make the appropriate sibling greetings. Then he began to fail. A congenital heart defect was discovered. Emergency surgery was done. The child died on his third day of life.

Our friends, whose faith came to the fore at this time, were struck. A funeral and burial were held within a few days. The child was buried in the Catholic cemetery in Cambridge. Because the parents were students, and had no permanent home they planned to go from there to wherever work would take them. In several years they would leave Cambridge and leave behind the body of the child they had welcomed so hopefully into the world.

The day of the burial was cold. It began to snow. Soft, wet flakes cascaded from the sky covering everything in sight. The funeral procession moved through the gathering snow out to the cemetery. Rushing flakes filled the dark earthen corners of the freshly dug grave, making a frozen lake in which the tiny coffin floated. A fine white mantle spread over the top as the coffin was lowered to the accompaniment of prayers. A more sobering form of water flowed that day than had immersed my son on the day of baptism.

Not all images of letting go are so gentle. Others are more fearful: family member missing, killed in a car accident, lost on the city streets of America to an unknown fate, estranged, dead of an overdose, suicide. Still others reflect a more normal experience of letting go that nonetheless challenges us: a child moving out, going away to college, getting married, making decisions a parent would not have made, children becoming parents themselves, parents aging, moving away. No matter what the scenario, letting go is a matter of reforming the heart that leads us deeper into the life of our God who is love.

To return to the story of our son's baptism, I must add that, to our associate pastor's credit, he and I did have several very fruitful, if heated, discussions about the incident at the morning liturgy. And he genuinely heard my pain when I said that our church rarely looks to the model of the family when it speaks of "welcoming." Rarely does a parish genuinely welcome its own children or teach them to embrace one another with anything even approaching the warmth of a parent's arms. Rarely are families given a language or a sense of the spiritual lessons to be culled from parenthood. Rarely does the Church speak to us of the heart of flesh that is being shaped within the deepest recesses of our being by our family. Rarely is the intimate attachment that recreates our hearts in the image of God's own unconditional love affirmed. Being family is a matter of hearts stretched and torn to love beyond our own selves. To welcome and then to let go of each other is to love like and to allow oneself to be loved by God.

·2·

We mark the coming and going of persons at the doorway. We also mark the movements of the seasons there. Christmas wreaths, Halloween pumpkins, May baskets, and birthday balloons decorate our doors to celebrate the cyclical and seasonal quality of existence that goes on within our homes. The family knows time in diverse ways; one is as an experience of moving always into the new: birth, growing up, new job, etc. We also know time as cyclical: a series of Christmases or Thanksgivings, each one linked to the others by the continuity of the family's very existence, one overlaid on the other as an unfolding story not only of the past but of the present and future as well. Time within the family simultaneously moves swiftly forward and stretches indolently back into the shared past and rests comfortably in a present that is at once utterly new and yet always the same. For the family's life spans time beyond the events of any individual member's life. Its story is both very old and very new.

The spirituality of family is not only concerned with recurring patterns, but also with the changing texture of the here and now; with the rapidly expanding minds and bodies of children; with the vigilance of maintaining healthy intimacy in marriage; with the challenges of young adulthood and mid-life; with birth and death.

The spiritual life of the family also spans the generations. Beyond the threshold of the door through which the ever-changing life of the family passes, is the hallway. Like the corridors in a medieval castle, the walls of the hallway are lined with the family's heraldry. Here the family identity is expressed in the dozens of faces that peer from photographs or painted portraits: a picture of the bride and groom, a snapshot of the first child in the arms of her aunt, a portrait with all the family members formally posed wearing their Sunday best, a picture of the high school prom, a college graduate in solemn black robes, grandparents standing in front of the farm back home, an uncle in military dress who died in a long-ago war.

The spiritual life of the family encompasses all these faces. An intertwining of destiny, of shared gifts, of collectively suffered pain makes the family a profoundly interdependent entity.

The stories that the hallway gallery illustrate serve as reminders of the family history: "This is who we are." "This is where we come from." "This is the home we have built." For anyone of the family's members to understand who he or she is, something of its story must be passed on and recounted within the family.

This telling of the unique stories is what creates a shared memory and identity and binds the family together: "All of us kids grew up on the farm, we used to get up before daylight to do chores and then walk five miles to school." "My grandparents were slaves, their struggle to become free is the struggle I inherit." "I escaped with my sisters and my mother from the old country where our people were being persecuted; when I came to America I couldn't speak a word of English." "We have been Americans since Colonial times." "All the men for four generations in our family have gone into the medical profession." "I never knew my father. He died in Vietnam." We know who we are because we know where we came from.

The individual's history becomes richer and more meaningful within the context of the family history. In turn, a new level of meaning is added to the family history by recalling the Christian story of which that family is a small part.

The photos in the hallway suggest moments in that multi-leveled narrative. The exchange of wedding vows, a baptism, or a confirmation are ritual moments that identify the family as Christian. More foundationally, these recorded moments serve to inform the family of its deepest identity. Beyond the knowledge that they are "American," "from the farm," or "from the old country," the family members know that they are children of a gracious and loving parent from whom they have come and to whom they will ultimately return. They are beloved sons and daughters, brothers and sisters of God's firstborn, called to love and care for each other with the same love and care that God lavishes on them.

A Time for Wonder

There is a season for everything, a time for every purpose under heaven.

Ecclesiastes 3:1

It is Advent. We have gathered around the table where our makeshift Advent wreath stands in the center. It is a pottery plate with three white votive candles and one red taper (I didn't have time to locate the liturgically correct purple and rose candles) nestled in a bed of evergreen now browning at the tips. We light the first two candles and read aloud the messianic passages from Isaiah which depict the peaceful coexistence of the lion and the lamb. We make it short. The baby is starting in on his evening fuss and my husband has a meeting that night.

Our brief question for shared reflection is, "How can I make my family life more peaceful this season?" My eldest daughter responds first with a look of wry humor (accompanied by a swift kick of the foot under the table), "Well, I suppose I could stop teasing my sister so much." My husband pauses, then announces that he could be a bit more relaxed about the proper use of implements ("No, you use a sponge, not a cloth napkin, to wipe up spills." "Do not use your teeth to open the lid of that can!"). I say I could practice delayed response and try not to react so emotionally to problems all the time. The baby's wailing has begun as he has dropped the sodden remains of an arrowroot biscuit onto the floor. He is too young to participate. My middle daughter, age three, has been pushing a ball of candle wax around the edge of the table. I am afraid she will knock something over.

My sense of the meeting is that we are ready to sing "O Come, O Come Emmanuel" and get on with our evening. But it seems unfair not to include her in the reflections. Not really expecting an answer, I turn to her and ask, "What do *you* think we should do to make our family a more peaceful place?" She pauses in her wax-rolling and looks up at us. Slowly she folds both hands in front of her and looks solemnly from face to face. "Watch for God," she answers.

Time is one medium given to us through which we can watch for God. And it is just that that we must do. We are, for the most part, like the foolish virgins of the Scriptures who did not watch for the bridegoom or the well-meaning disciples who fell asleep in the Garden of Gethsemane while Jesus kept his last and lonely vigil in prayer. We do not watch for God. We do not live in the expectation that God will suddenly become present to us, right here and now. And yet that is what we are invited to expect. Time—this present time—is given to us to watch for God.

Times of the Gathered Church

There are so many ways in which time can become transformed into an experience of watching. These ways spread across the spectrum of experience, from those recognized and celebrated by the entire gathered Christian community to those unique to each person and family. As a gathered people we observe sacred times and seasons—the liturgical calendar—during which we watch for God through the eyes of Scripture and tradition. During Advent we anticipate the first coming of God enfleshed in the manger at Bethlehem. We also look to the Second Coming foretold in the striking seasonal readings drawn from the Book of Revelation. And lastly, we celebrate the constant birth of God in our own hearts and midst.

During Lent we fast and discipline ourselves, bringing to consciousness our limitations and our need for God. We approach the mystery of human suffering, both personal and collective, as people of the question. We do not seek answers but begin to anticipate answers in our struggle to heal the wounds, expose the violence, and create a place for God in our hearts. At Pentecost we acknowledge our being-in-community, the mystery of church that speaks of more-than-human solidarity and which is animated by the Spirit of God that infuses each and all of us with life.

The power of the varied sacred times and rituals of the liturgical year to awaken us to watchfulness is immense. I will never approach Maundy Thursday without remembering one time several years ago when we spent Holy Week and Easter in Baltimore with dear friends who were worshiping at a small Episcopal parish where the husband of the couple served as music minister. We sat through the worship service, I somewhat distracted by my wiggling toddler who insisted on removing the hymnals from their casings and trying to fit them in again. My attention, however, was arrested by what began to take place at the end of the service.

As the chords of the final hymn died away, the church became still and quiet. No one moved to leave. The lights gradually went down. A man and a woman from the congregation came forward and began the measured and solemn ritual of stripping the altar. I had never seen this ritual performed with such power to move. Perhaps because the church was a modern one with no statuary, or ornament attached to the structure itself, the stripping became quite dramatic. Piece by piece, each article of worship was taken away until only a void was left in this darkened space, where only minutes before we had been part of the gathering of Jesus and his friends at supper. A simple wooden cross was placed on the bare altar and carefully shrouded in black cloth. My children were transfixed. The entire congregation sat for a long time in the darkness, eyes fixed on the dim light that illuminated the covered cross. Then slowly they began to leave the church and move silently out into the night. I never experienced so vividly the movement from the Last Supper to the Garden of Gethsemane where

Jesus wept in lonely agony and asked his disciples to watch with him. "Stay here and keep watch with me." The words hung in the stillness.

We too left the church in silence. The night sky of spring was flecked with stars. The sharp retort of scattered gravel overturned by our feet was the only sound heard. We remained silent for most of the drive home until my eldest daughter leaned over against me and said in a low urgent voice, "I want to stay awake all night. I won't abandon him. I will watch too."

The great seasons of the liturgical year are, at least to some degree, lived by most Christians. But the calendar is also filled with minor observances, rich in history and imagery, that can transform the flat landscapes of our lives into mountaintop moments. How few of us celebrate the seasons given to watch for God, seasons full of wonder.

The marvelous thing about the year is that it is cyclical. We come round to the varied feasts each year and so our experience becomes layered, made richer by the return of days which hold for us memories and meanings of our own and our community's spiritual odyssey. I have many of these days which, upon their return, serve not only to remind me of the goodness of God's care but also of who I am—part of a people called by God. And each year the themes celebrated on a given day unfold with nuance and added meaning contoured by the circumstances of the new year.

I first came alive to the feast of the Presentation many years ago (before marriage and children) when I was making a prolonged retreat at a Trappestine monastery. In many ways the retreat's focus was vocational discernment. I had no special expectation for this day, until I was roused early to join in a candlelight procession at dawn. White-robed and bearing torches, the community and I threaded our way from the outside of the monastery confines through the building's hallways and into the chapel. The ceremony bespoke the presentation of our lives to the Lord, just as the infant Jesus had been presented at the Temple, the requisite offering to God of the firstborn son. In that growing dawn, our only light the flickering flames from our torches, we offered ourselves wholly to God, each of us placing our candles on the altar. Each year as that feast returns I remember that offering and surrender myself anew to the arms of the Lord, just as Mary surrendered her child to the arms of the priest Simeon. And I try to remember the promises God made of old, promises of joy and peace and hope, and to remember that the offering is made for all people.

Times of the Domestic Church

The liturgical year is our gathered community's means of wonder, marking the times through which we as a people watch for God. Families can participate in these great times in their own ways. They can create or borrow rituals that suit their own lifestyles and life stages.[1] They can observe not only Lent, Easter, Advent, and Christmas, but special saints' days and the anniversaries of baptismal days. Even so simple a ritual as bringing out the baptismal candle or the white infant's garment worn on the day of baptism, sharing memories while looking at pictures in the family album, makes this a special family time of watching for God.

Beyond the specific Christian days and seasons that the family commemorates, there are sacred times that emerge organically from each family's life. Birthdays are an obvious example. Families can transform each birthday into a blessed one by truly making it a day of remembrance and welcome, a day when the honored one is reminded of how essential he or she is to the whole. It is a time for the family to become a people of the story. Perhaps the story of the day of the child's birth can be retold each year over the breakfast table. Perhaps pictures from former birthday celebrations will be brought out. In remembering, especially within the context of our community, be it family or parish, we learn who we are. For our individual stories are part of our family's story, and our family story is part of the story of our being brought to birth by God. We come into life through the waters and blood of our mother's bodies and to a new life through the blood and waters of the body of Jesus.

There are sacred times unique to each family. Usually they are times when everyone is present, when all are genuinely *present* to each other, times set aside when the hurry and fragmentation of daily life gives way to a time that is less future-oriented and goal-directed. Vacations and days off are often sacred times for families. A weekend in the cabin in the mountains, an afternoon at a favorite picnic spot by a stream, a day off when we wash the car together and walk unhurriedly down to the soda fountain for a milkshake, an evening when we lie on our stomachs on the big waterbed and play games, the yearly springtime ritual of looking for the first crocus, particular smells and tastes of Sunday afternoon dinner with grandparents, Saturday morning when dad fixes pancakes, family reunions. The variations are as numerous as the families themselves.

There is a distinctive quality to these times. They are times not narrowed by our usual attitude of seeing time as a slim corridor through which we are speeding and which never allows us enough space to do everything that we think must be done to get ready for some future time. Family's sacred days and seasons are expansive. They are time to allow for surprise and discovery. Often they are a time of play. They are times when lingering and listening and seeing with new eyes is possible.

Not Enough Time

In a recent survey taken among U.S. Catholics it was time (or the seeming lack of it) that was seen as the major factor that inhibited the cultivation of a rich family spirituality.[2] Most of our lives are exhaustingly filled with work, chores, school, extra-curricular activities, hobbies, clubs, meetings, sports, social activities, personal enrichment, and charitable works. We keep calendars and coordinate schedules. Much of our busyness is forced on us by economic necessity. Some of it is part of our social malaise. One survey reports that American families often do not even sit down to one meal a day together because of someone's soccer game, another's ballet rehearsal, a third's commitment to the church fundraiser, or a fourth's inescapable business meeting.

Indeed the gathered church body often encourages us, as committed Christians, to fill our time with "meaningful" activities. But the very emphasis on the church's family programing, especially when it is geared for each age and interest group, becomes a force that fragments the family. A story was recounted to me not long ago of a parish council meeting at which a proposal was being considered for adding a recreation facility to the church plant. Put forward as a great ministry to families, an elaborate array of possible program offerings was suggested. One mother of three teenagers went against the tide of enthusiasm for the new gym. The gym and the proposed programs would divide her family, she said. Monday night she would chauffeur son number one to the seniors' Christian basketball league, Tuesday her husband would disappear with the men's support group, Wednesday son number two would have to be shuttled back and forth for juniors' Christian basketball, her daughter would have been shuttled earlier that same afternoon for Pre-teens Encounter Christ, Thursday the Ladies' Auxiliary would pressure her to work out with "Praisercise," and then on Saturday everyone would be gone in different directions for the fundraising meeting, boy's hobby club, the girl's glee, the bake sale, and the Youth Camping Association. She was not sure the suggestions before the parish council could be considered ministering to families if you conceived as a family as anything more than its discrete parts.

Her point is well taken. Our family lives need time of wonder. These are difficult to find when we are frantic with activity and separated from one another in the process. We do not need to be hermits to experience the deep disclosure of presence and sacred time available to us when we play unpurposefully together, when we are silent together on a meander through the forest, or when we simply sit and enjoy the gentle lapping of the ocean as we lie on the beach and with our fingers make furrows in the sand.

Time is one medium given us in which to watch for God. God is there when we are genuinely present to one another. When there is time for a conversation over a pot of tea, to sit on the edge of a bed and share the small sorrows of the day, to stop and collect a cluster of dandelions, to marvel at the miracle of each other, there is time for wonder and time to watch for God.

·3·

The doorway and hallway, as liminal structures, articulate the internal family experience of welcoming and leave-taking. They also speak of these dynamics practiced in relation to those outside the family circle. The doorway proclaims that hospitality, the most ancient of Christian practices, is part of the home's spiritual life. This is the sacred space where the family opens itself to friend or stranger. Hospitality has a long history in church life and was one of the express ideals of early monasticism. The *Rule of St. Benedict* says:

> All guests who present themselves are to be welcomed as Christ, for he himself will say: I was a stranger and you welcomed me. Proper honor must be shown to all.... Great care and concern are to be shown in receiving poor people and pilgrims, because in them more particularly Christ is received. (Chap. 53)

Benedictine monastic grounds generally include a guest facility where visitors are welcomed, invited to participate in the liturgical life of the community, and be refreshed in the spirit of silence and prayer pervading the environs.

Hospitality in such a context is an open-armed embrace of a fellow child of God, a recognition of the ties of mutual care that bind the community together and mark it as Christian. In analogous fashion, the family home "makes room" for the guest who is always awaited. Parlors and living rooms are the spaces within the home that have the special function of hospitably embracing guests. These may be quite formal (one thinks of the old-fashioned parlor with carefully arranged chairs that one never sat on save for the express purpose of receiving) where the family "goes out" to greet visitors. Or they may be rather informal, perhaps a cozy living space crowded with an overstuffed sofa and some beanbag pillows, where the guest is incorporated into the ongoing bustle of the residents' lives. Whatever the style, these are the sacred spaces within the home where hospitality is experienced as spiritual practice and gift.

The Christ-Room

By now they were nearing the village (of Emmaus) to which
they were going and he acted as if he were going farther.
But they pressed him: "Stay with us. It is evening and the
day is practically over." So he went in to stay with them.

When he had seated himself with them to eat, he took
bread, pronounced the blessing, then broke it and began to
distribute it to them. With that their eyes were opened and
they recognized him.

Luke 24:28–31

As I reflect on hospitality within the family, one graced experience in my own life stands out. Several years ago I was asked to be part of a weekend consultation in a city partway across the country. I really wanted to accept, but at the time our youngest child was only several months old and still a nursing baby. To leave him abruptly for the long weekend that the trip required was, for me, unthinkable. The only possibility other than simply not going was to take him with me. The sponsors of the project agreed and graciously offered to provide babysitting backup for the actual hours of the consultation. I was pleased that such a congenial arrangement could be made.

I was also, in fact, a bit apprehensive about the prospect of trying to straddle the two worlds of domestic and professional attentiveness. How would the baby do in a new place? Would I be sleepless and bleary-eyed, distracted when I heard him cry? Would he panic in the care of a stranger? Would I be a washout at this consultation? Would I be trapped in a hotel or dorm room where a baby's cries would disturb others? Would my milk supply be affected by the disturbance of the trip?

I got on the plane with the vast paraphenalia necessary in this culture to provide for an infant and simply surrendered myself to whatever might happen. We weathered two flights and change of planes pretty well, but when we arrived at our destination, we discovered that our luggage had not arrived. In fact, the cases had been flown elsewhere. The airline company said apologetically that it might be a day or two before they could be tracked down.

Fortunately we were greeted not only with this bleak news but also by our host, the consultation organizer. He saw our plight and began to remedy the situation. We were whisked away from the airport and taken to his home, a comfortable ranch-style house out in the country. He and his wife, a childless couple who had married a bit later than usual, had arranged for us to stay with them. I soon learned that this remarkable couple—she an ordained minister and he a theological school graduate—had entered into their marriage after a period of serious reflection about whether marriage was indeed the vocation to which they each separately and together were called. After discerning that indeed God was inviting them to enflesh the Christian life through marriage, they reflected together upon the disciplines of that life particular to family. At the top of their list was hospitality—not just entertaining lots of friends, but genuine, Christian hospitality, the creation of a space, both physical and spiritual, a room that invites the guest to enter and feel genuinely welcome and "at home." The deepest dimension of hospitality is realized when each visitor is recognized as the Christ, when each traveler is refreshed from the journey not only by the comforts of food and rest, but by the delightful experience of being appreciated and valued for the God-given uniqueness of his or her person.

Even before I learned about this couple's conscious decision to live this kind of hospitality, I felt it in their home. I have been in many welcoming environments, been made comfortable and cherished by many families. But this was special. They had set aside a room for hospitality. This was not the typical guest room which is either the spare room at the back of the house, unused since a child went away to college, or a room which otherwise functions as a sewing room, or a den that has a bed or foldout couch. This was a room expressly meant for the guest. The favored location suggested that the original architect has intended it for use as a master bedroom suite.

There was nothing ostentatious or even elegant about the appointments of this guest room. It was furnished rather simply but with great care. I had the distinct sense that this couple had stood in the room and thought carefully about all the small details that would delight guests and make them feel at home. There was a handmade bowl filled with potpourri, an antique petit point pillow nestled in the arm of an old rocking chair. There was nothing particular about what was there, but everything spoke surely, "*You* are welcome." This room was *so* different from a hotel suite with its generic furnishings. It was even distinct from a bed-and-breakfast establishment that, as quaint and unique as one might be, is still a commercial venture, comfort provided in exchange for pay. This was a world away from such an atmosphere. In their home they created a space within that awaited and celebrated the unrepeatable presence of each guest.

My host found out at the airport that I would not have a change of clothes for the next day's consultation and telephoned ahead to his wife who, as fortune would have it, was about my size. In my closet hung a variety of dresses to be looked over. In the chest of drawers was a nightgown and slips and everything else I could have needed. A box of disposable diapers was also there (my host had also ascertained that I had several changes of clothes for the baby in the diaper bag I was carrying). I ate dinner with this couple that evening, we chatted casually in the kitchen while he chopped vegetables and she set the table with linen. Their hospitality was at once special yet never stuffy. The baby with his spit-up and fingers grasping at the edges of the cloth seemed perfectly in place. Needless to say, my worries about the consultation were completely dispelled. Both my son and I slept wonderfully and woke to gentle sunlight streaming through the windows.

On Sunday morning the couple suggested several local churches we might attend (theirs was a ecumenical marriage) and presented the option of staying home and informally praying the liturgy together. We decided to do the latter. We gathered on their back porch overlooking a sloping green meadow that was rimmed by a forest of low trees. The day was bright but breezy. The husband and I shared readings from the Scriptures. The wife presided at our worship. The baby added his gurgles to the reflections. We broke bread together, were silent together, sang a wonderful, moving old hymn together.

When I left their home I carried away with me a heightened sense of one facet of the Christian family's vocation, the spirit of hospitality.[1]

Celebrating the Guest

As families we can extend the gift of hospitality in many ways. Not all of us can easily equip an entire suite for the guest. But all of us can welcome others and share with them the love and warmth that is generated among ourselves. Styles of hospitality will vary from family to family, but I think it important that we distinguish it from "entertaining." The point is not to create an elaborate display of culinary delights or to impress guests with polite social etiquette. Hospitality has little to do with showing off your newly redecorated living room or bringing out the sterling silver service. Welcoming visitors, making them aware of their value and the special gift of presence they bring is what is essential. Hospitality means including the guest in the family circle with the knowledge that as our eyes are opened we begin to recognize Christ in them.

While all of us like to have things in good order when guests arrive and all of us do need to honor the legitimate desire for family privacy, still genuine hospitality pushes us beyond these considerations. One young wife I knew confided in me that she and her husband had given up having people in since the birth of their second child. No, things were simply too chaotic and unpredictable to try to deal with children's bedtimes, doing things "the way they ought to be done." I later learned (after her youngest child had reached the more rational age of five) that her idea of receiving guests was elaborate, formal dining that involved serving gourmet dishes that took all day to prepare. While her meals were delicious, her attitude to guests is expressed better as "entertaining" than "hospitality." The focus was on how her home and meals would measure up to her own very high standards and expectations.

A hospitable attitude, in contrast, is other-oriented in a positive way, focusing on the needs of the other and delighting in the particularity of *person* that the other brings. Expressions of hospitality can run the gamut from the frequent receiving of intimate friends who are "just like family," to the more formal opening of the house to neighbors or business associates, social club members or prayer groups.

Whatever the form, hospitality within the domestic church engenders a sense of celebration and play. The family may plan a surprise birthday for an unsuspecting friend or make their home a place of reception following the baptism of a new godchild. They may regularly set aside Sunday afternoons for prayer and reflection with another family. They may offer a room and meals to visitors from out of town, taking them on a tour of the city. Or they may simply invite friends over on the spur of the moment to celebrate some good news with a dish of ice cream or a bottle of champagne. Their home may become a favorite refuge for a single friend living far from family who is enlivened by the unpredictable quality of life with small children. Or it may become known as a joyful place where the cumulative comings and goings of many persons have created a palpable atmosphere of hospitality. The family that makes space and takes time for others is enriched immeasurably in return.

A Christ-Room

A radical vision of Christian hospitality and one that might inspire families underlies the vision of the Catholic Worker movement founded in this country by Dorothy Day and Peter Maurin. A philosophy of personalism pervades the Worker and gives it a special spirit. For the founders of this movement, the Christian mission consists in re-envisioning and reshaping the imagination of society to give primary value to the God-given dignity and value of each human life. This task can only be realized when we see the commonality of our life together. Christ is to be seen and welcomed in each unique person. As Christians practice the traditional corporal works of mercy (feeding the hungry, giving drink to the thirsty, clothing the naked, visiting the imprisioned, sheltering the homeless, visiting the sick, and burying the dead) we show that we have understood the meaning of Christ's plaint, "I was hungry and you gave me no food, I was thirsty and you gave me no drink. I was away from home and you gave me no welcome" (Matthew 25:42–43). Each person has the responsibility to respond to each person he or she encounters in a spirit of genuine hospitality—welcoming him or her as the Christ.

One of the ways the Catholic Worker Movement enfleshed this ideal was to create Houses of Hospitality where the poor, the hungry, and the homeless would be greeted as guest, where the special story of each person's life could be recognized, spoken, and heard. This radical welcome of the person as Christ is reflected in the words of Dorothy Day.

> I watched that ragged horde and thought to myself, "these are Christ's poor. He was one of them. He was a man like other men and He chose His friends amongst the ordinary workers."[2]
>
> . . . There is our House of Hospitality. Ours, of course, is like a large family and when the women come to us they come for an indefinite stay. Some of them have been with us for the past four years. We have no rules, any more than the average family has, and we ask no questions. Many of the women have come to us so exhausted by poverty and insecurity it has taken them months to recover. There are others who will always be victims

of shattered nerves, and incapable of holding down any job.
Many of them try to help us in the work around the house.
Whatever cooperation they give is voluntary.[3]

Perhaps the practices of families that most approximate this vision of hospitality are adoption, especially of the disabled or dis-
placed child; opening our homes to shelter a homeless couple, a
pregnant unwed teen, or a young person estranged from their
own family; becoming family for a time for a foreign exchange
student or foster child. These radical forms of welcome require
the family to really "open its eyes" to see the Christ-presence in
the figure of the guest.

All forms of hospitality that genuinely emerge from a sense of
inviting and greeting the guest as one would Jesus himself share
in the Worker spirit. Dorothy Day once wrote, "The first unit of
society is the family. The family should look after its own and, in
addition, as the early Fathers said, 'Every home should have a
Christ-room in it so that the hospitality may be practiced.' "[4]

Christian families must have arms wide enough and hearts big
enough to create a space in which others are welcomed and, by
that welcome, come to know their deepest identity as children
of God.

·4·

Once we have passed beyond the entry and receiving areas of the home, we find ourselves in those spaces where the family gathers to enact the rituals of its life together. These spaces, whose central location and spaciousness expresses the commonality of the life contained, are places of meeting, gathering, and celebrating.

The dining room or the kitchen, depending on the home, especially can become for a family the sacred location of commonality. Whenever I have taught a class or done a workshop on family spirituality, I ask the participants to name the sacred places of their families' lives. Inevitably the first answer I receive is "the dinner table." Dinnertime is not necessarily perceived as a place of solemnity and holiness (although I have heard some people say there was a special way of "being" at their family's table—ritual rules as it were). Rather, the fact that at the dinner table the family gathers together and enacts the ritual of being a community of mutual need and nourishment in the sharing of food makes this experience sacred.

To prepare and share a meal together is one of the holiest acts in all religious traditions. Food and its preparation often are part of the ritual and taboo of a people's religious life. What one may or may not eat distinguishes the practitioner: a Jew must observe kosher dietary restrictions just as a Hindu may not consume beef or a Muslim pork. Certain foods are associated with certain seasons: in Christian circles, the observance of Lent involves periodic abstinence from flesh meat, and the Jewish seder is celebrated by preparing a shank of lamb and unleavened bread. These customs have significance for the self-understanding of the adherents of these various traditions. They point to the meal as a sacred event. The production and preparation of food is one of humankind's essential activities. To eat is to sustain life. To eat together is to sustain life in community.

Only very recently in human history, and only in our industrialized society, has the bulk of the food consumed not also been grown, harvested, and prepared by the same hands that eat it. Only in our land of almost scandalous abundance can we easily forget the wonder and gratitude that belongs to most of our brothers and sisters as they consume the daily fare that keeps them alive on this earth.

For the most part we have lost our sense of the urgency and power of hunger. We have lost our sense of the intense labor involved in the production of food. We have lost our sense of the gift and fragility of the earth that must be tended with love so that we can sustain our own lives. All this impoverishes our sense of what it is to break bread together.

Yet the communion with one another that takes place when we gather and share space, thoughts, and concerns as well as food, is still known in families today. We may not always be aware of it. We may not often gather together to share a meal. We may pass our meals in conflict or with trivial conversation. Yet the power of the ritual remains. At the deepest level, the gathering in the dining room or at the kitchen table is an experience of communion in which the mystery of our mutual need and nourishment is played out. This is the level of our true hunger and satiety and the level on which we must encounter one another to genuinely know who we are.

Body of Christ

And how . . . should you and others look upon the mystery
[of the body and blood] and touch it? Not only with your
bodily eyes and feeling, for here they would fail you. You
know that all your eyes see is this bit of bread; this is all
your hand can touch and all your tongue can taste, so your
bodily senses are deceived. . . . How then is this sacrament
touched? With the hand of love . . . You must receive this
sacrament not only with your bodily senses but with your
spiritual sensitivity, by disposing your soul to see and
receive and taste this sacrament with affectionate love.

St. Catherine of Siena, "The Mystic Body
of Holy Church" from *The Dialogues*

When I was a little girl I had a favorite poem, a humorous
lyric by E. V. Wright entitled "When Father Carves the Duck."
The poem depicts a family ritual-event at which the father pre-
sides. In it his solemn, becoming-grim-then-ferocious wrestling
with a fowl that he is trying to dismember is wonderfully described. The last verse caps the scene:

> We then have learned to walk around
>   the dining room and pluck
> From off the window sills and walls
>   our share of father's duck.
> While father growls and blows and jaws
> And swears the knife was full of flaws
> And mother laughs at him because
> He couldn't carve a duck.[1]

This poem always reminded me of my own father's presiding at
the family table. And I am still fond of hauling out these verses to

read aloud on Thanksgiving or Christmas when our own table sports a fowl to be similarly attacked and dismembered. It speaks to me not only of the half-amusing, half-nostalgic moments of my upbringing but also of the way most of us, myself topping the list, go about being in community. Some of us attack it from a position of splendidly armed and determined isolation. We know ourselves to be problem-solvers, to be in opposition to life and the "others" that the hapless fowl represents. Some of us are passive and opportunistic scavengers who pluck from off the window sills and walls of life the leftover and fragmentary pieces of nourishment that we can. A few enlightened souls find the resources simply to laugh at the whole debacle.

The greatest lessons I have learned as a familied person have been those of community. Not only have I learned to exist reasonably (or not so reasonably) under the same roof with a variety of personalities, not only have I learned that it takes time and effort and communication skills to negotiate in community, I also have learned that at the root of community there is the mystery of communion, the mystery that together we are the body of Christ.

One of the things that surprised me most about getting married and having a family is that the whole is more than the parts. There is a reality to "us" as a family that transcends the individuals in it. This is true in terms of the dynamic interactions. It is also true of the spirit that animates a family's interior life. I first became aware of this through the experience of marriage. I have been married twice. The first one failed, in part at least, because neither of us was really aware of or attentive to the fact that there was an entity existing greater than either of our individual interests or concerns. Not that we did not do things together, but we did them mainly with a sense of "you" and "me" and not with sensitivity to that elusive and powerful third presence that is born when a marriage comes into being. I have struggled in my second marriage to dance the intricate choreography of "you," "me," and "us," and to maintain a flexible enough deportment to lean toward or away from any one of these realities as the music of the moment requires.

The same is true of a family. The whole is greater than the parts. One of my children's picture books has put this succinctly into the mouth of a mother raccoon shown holding a newborn in her arms and trying to cushion the jealousy of an older sibling, "Goodness knows, I like babies. But a baby isn't a family. A family is everybody all together." Our all-togetherness has a special life and quality all its own.

Family therapists refer to such a transindividual entity as the "family ego." Often in their opinion this is conceived as something that one should avoid being engulfed in. I wonder if there is also a "family spirit" into which we as separate persons enter, not to the dimunition of our own distinctiveness but to our enhancement.

I would hope that we as Christians could cultivate a view of family that is more expansive than the ones that dominate our popular culture. From that perspective, families are seen as either a potential hindrance to individual development (i.e., one must be careful to define one's "space") or, conversely, families are seen as entities to which all individuality must be submerged. (I once read in a Christian family magazine of a woman who said she was committed to really *giving herself* to her family; that meant spending almost all her time shuttling her two sons back and forth to their 100-plus athletic events per school year. I found myself wondering what qualities of her self had been given to her sons in her commitment.)

I prefer to view the family as a genuine community that both promotes the full individuation of its members yet calls upon the participation and loving energy of all to continue existence. In this cooperation something mysterious and powerful is created that transcends and enlivens the members of that community.

What this brings to mind is the passage in which Jesus claims, "Where two or more of you are gathered, there am I also" (Matt. 18:20).[2] There is something about our all-togetherness that is much more than conviviality. Our togetherness, when it is fully realized, is a state of being that, I think, approaches the divine in whose image we are made. For God does not create in the way a machine manufactures innumerable discrete and identical pieces. Rather, we are part of life itself, an organic whole that sustains us and to which we contribute in an essential way. In the complex, beautifully articulated organism that is this ecosystem, human beings are irreplaceable and contributing parts.

Authentic human community exists in this manner as well. We live fully when we live with and for each other, when we recognize that our individuality contributes to and is enhanced by the rest of the community. And the whole of our togetherness is more than the parts, for the *whole* reveals God's extraordinary creative capacity. Yet the whole never obscures or denies the unique and irreplaceable quality of each. When we break bread together we symbolically enact the basic truth that we *are* most complete when we are together.

Together. Community. Nice words. I think we all hunger for the sustenance of genuine loving community. Our Christian history is full of attempts, some successful, some not, to live out in practical ways the full mystery of our communal life. And always at the center of our shared worship has been a meal that ritually enacts for us the deepest level of our community—the level of communion.

What does it mean to be in communion with one another? It means more than to gather. It means that we share our lives at levels of which most of us are only dimly aware. It means that we are mutually dependent upon one another. It means that my needs and another's gifts and my gifts and another's needs are like parts of an unassembled jigsaw puzzle. Until they are fitted together the puzzle cannot be complete. It means that our need and caring are cause for celebration. If we could overcome the isolation of our hearts, we would discover a larger self than the one we hide from need and caring.

I don't think I ever really appreciated the sense of communion that is implicit in the ritual of the Eucharist until the time I was asked to be part of a parish retreat's leadership team. The focus for several days was upon linking individual spirituality to the wider Christian community. I was asked to do the opening segment and give the retreatants an opportunity to reflect on their own personal relationships with God. Because I like to be concrete when I do retreats, I accompanied my talk with the making of the bread that was to be served at the eucharistic service that would end our time together. The ingredients—flour, water, salt,—were, I suggested, the stuff of our lives: our time, talent, prayers, loves, hopes, actions. These we bring to our life as community. As I talked, I measured out, combined the ingredients, and formed them into loaves. These were allowed to sit for some time and then were baked.

I was not prepared for what I experienced at the eucharistic service the next day. There was the bread that I had made with my own hands, which I had so self-consciously described as the very stuff of my/our own lives. When the time came for the consecration and the bread was lifted up, blessed, and broken, all of the elements of my own and all the retreatants' lives seemed lifted up, blessed and broken, passed out, and consumed in a meal of mutual exchange. I had never before felt so vividly our own sacrificial participation with the man Jesus in whose memory and presence we celebrate this rite. Nor had I ever felt how much the very substance of our lives is given, and consumed, not for our individual salvation, but for and by the whole community, nor how much others' substances provide the nourishment through which we are each sustained.

To be in communion also means that when we open ourselves to become aware of our shared life and to live accordingly, we genuinely begin to be one body. And that one body is greater than any separate part. We are the body of Christ. The mystery of our communion is that we are daughters and sons of God with and in Christ. Present in our gathering, in our becoming a *people,* not just an assembly of separate persons, is another, greater presence. This presence can only be there when we allow ourselves to acknowledge our mutual need and nourishment, when we bring the fullness of who we are to be gift for each other and to be recipients of each other's gifts.

There are ways of being together in family that do not approach the experience of communion. We can be one or two over against the other(s). We can be codependents in abusive relationships that thwart our individuality and shared growth. We can be locked into rigid systems of dominance and oppression. But the other possibility is there. For healing. For growth. For the emergence of true community and true communion.

We need the courage to admit our own needfulness, our own hunger for the tender care that genuine community can bring. We need the courage to cry out and confront when abuses exist in our families. We need the humility to admit our shortcomings and to ask forgiveness from God and one another.

We need to come to the shared table that is our life and to break bread together. We need to feed each other and be fed. In this consists the mystery of our communion. In this we *are* the body of Christ.

·5·

The furniture located in the common rooms of most homes is, for the most part, movable. There may be a sofa or an arrangement of chairs in the living room or parlor that defines the area designated for the gathering of the family and guests. In most homes these formal settings are expanded or rearranged as the need arises. This is true of the dining area as well. Extra chairs, children's and infants' seats, an additional leaf to the table are added or subtracted depending upon who is present at a given mealtime or according to the expanding size of family over the years.

There is likewise furniture that defines the gathering of smaller units of family. There may be a love seat in a corner of the front room that invites intimate conversation between two people alone. Or there may be a kitchen stool that becomes the place where each child sits after returning home from school or work to relate the tale of today's adventure outside the confines of home. The furniture in most homes has a way of expressing the relationships that go on inside. Every range of family structure is represented—from far apart and never yielding, to crowded in next to each other and ever-shifting.

The dynamics of the family life are similar. This is not simply a question of numbers of bodies to be housed; the spirit life of family is discovered in how close, how far, how interconnected and copenetrating those bodies are to become.

I find it fascinating that in a course I taught to a mixed group of celibate, married, single, and familied people, one of the characteristics of family spirituality that my students singled out was the characteristic of touch. The spirituality of family, they insisted, has much to do with the experience of touching and being touched in all the ways in which those terms are commonly understood—physically, emotionally, intellectually, and spiritually. I agree. I am also aware that the spirituality we inherit from our wider tradition has given little attention to the phenomenon of touching and being touched. In fact, until quite recently, the physical and emotional aspects of human touching have as a rule been either ignored or disdained as part of the life of the spirit.[1]

But the spirit that moves among the members of the body of Christ enfleshed in family is a spirit most vividly known through touch. We move toward or away from each other. We occupy together the love seat, or we sit apart in chairs placed in far corners of the room. The arts of moving closer and farther away from one another are at the root spiritual arts. Who, when, and how we touch and are touched—spiritually, intellectually, physically, and emotionally—is of utmost importance. For the whole of the body is only realized when all the parts are in communion with one another, when each is open and responsive to be touched by others and when others are able to touch in a manner that reflects a sensitivity to the dignity of each created person and their unique contribution to the whole.

Life in family as a spiritual discipline is like the careful and continual rearrangement of the furniture in the common rooms of our home: closer together or farther away; more or less; side by side or face to face; intimate groupings or seating for a crowd; formal or casual arrangements. The variations are endless. The spirit never rests.

A Way That You Know Not

To come to the pleasure you have not
  You must go by a way in which you enjoy not
To come to the knowledge you have not
  You must go by a way which you know not
To come to the possession you have not
  You must go by a way in which you possess not
To come to what you are not
  You must go by a way in which you are not.

St. John of the Cross, Sketch of
the *Ascent of Mount Carmel*

I was fortunate enough during the period following the breakup of my first marriage to share the friendship of another person who was experiencing the same process. It was helpful to be in the presence of someone whose life was similarly thrown into chaos and to have my own perspective enlarged by one whose perceptions of that chaos were not always the same. His divorce was a rather simple event, as these things go. There were no children, no common property, or disagreement about the rightness of severing what was the fiction of a marriage.

One day, I happened quite inadvertently to be in the kitchen of the apartment this couple had shared. My friend opened a drawer to take out a spoon for the coffee he was preparing. I gradually realized he had stopped moving and had frozen while looking into that drawer. Tears welled up and he began to weep uncontrollably. "Spoons," he managed to say. There in the place where his ex-wife had kept a set of silver teaspoons, was nothing but empty space.

The experience of absence where there had been presence is a fearful thing. Any genuine love, any real intimacy, creates a presence that is a permanent reality in one's life. No matter what the future of a relationship, if it is of any substance, if the partners have touched and been touched, an imprint is made that remains. When death or divorce severs the bonds of intimacy, an imprint is left which cannot but be felt.

Singleness, as opposed to marriage or vowed celibacy, is a state in life for which our Church has little appreciation. There certainly is no articulated spirituality of singleness, nor is there a place in the institution for Christians who find their lives mirrored neither in the home life of the familied nor in the community life or public ministry of the celibate person.[1] Yet many Christians are single either because they have never been or are no longer committed in either marriage or religious life. And many of our Christian families are headed by women or men who find themselves in the sometimes lonely and perplexing circumstance of single parenthood. For many there has been a partner, a presence in their lives, that now exists as an empty drawer. Their voices need to be heard and the special spirituality that emerges from their particular lifestyles and concerns must become part of our shared wisdom if we are to be a Church whose spiritual life is a living and compassionate one.

Parenting Alone

My own experience with single parenting is very limited. I cannot speak with the ring of authenticity that might characterize the speech of others who have lived that vocation for many years. My first marriage was childless; its termination affected only me. Yet I do know a little bit about being a single parent, especially in its logistical aspects. By dabbling my feet into its waters I have sensed the formidable currents that are there. Several years ago, after my husband had nearly completed a course of studies in the town where we had moved for precisely that purpose, he was offered a job in another part of the country. This was exactly the type of position he had hoped for, and all the other factors that had to be calculated in such a move were agreeable to all of us. Only the job started six months too soon. I was teaching. Our children were in school and in a good cooperative day care. It was the dead of winter and we had no place to move into. We decided my husband should take the job. The kids and I would follow in the spring.

I learned many things from the months I was the sole caregiver for our children. Because of the distance and expense, my husband was only able to return a few times for what were in essence long weekend visits. I learned, first of all, what an immense task parenting is when shouldered alone. I learned too how nearly impossible it is to "share" parenting with others who have no relationship to your children.

I was in the enviable position of having a large community of people around me from the institution to which we were attached, many of whom offered to help out once they knew that I was to be alone for a time. I figured that by parceling out the responsibilities my husband had undertaken, I at least could manage to get through those months without too much wear and tear. Four people volunteered to drive my eldest across town to school in the mornings on a rotating shift. (It was impossible for me to do that and get my younger two children to day care before I had to be at work.) Another friend would take her to flute lessons on the afternoon when I was teaching. A second would pick her up from Brownies on the afternoon when I had to be in another part of town picking up the little kids at the day care. Someone in the building offered to take out the trash which had to be hauled down many flights of stairs and out into the snow, a task that was difficult with an infant and a toddler who could not be left alone. Occasionally folks would volunteer to pick something up at the store or to babysit when I had a meeting to attend or when a child fell ill. One faithful friend even agreed to come for the weekend on which I was out of town for a talk and conference. In the beginning it seemed straightforward enough.

What I didn't anticipate was the relentless nature of the needs that emerged in our family once one parent was gone. All my helpers were enthusiastic in the beginning. Midway through they began to feel the strain. Getting up at 6:30 A.M. as a gesture of sheer charity every Thursday when they had exams pending or were planning a jaunt out of town was hard. I began to wear them out with the needs that I couldn't meet myself. I began to feel like a beggar. I stopped asking my faithful volunteers and asked others to help. I hated the feeling of having to ask for favors constantly. I felt humiliated and a burden on all those people whose generosity had been so great.

I remember hitting bottom one winter's day when I had stayed home, bringing my class preparation with me, to be with my daughter who was sick in bed with a hundred-and-three degree fever. Somehow I had managed to drive the other kids elsewhere that morning after I asked a neighbor in the next apartment to sit with the invalid for three-quarters of an hour. When the time came to pick them up, there was no one in our apartment building. The temperature outside had dropped to subzero and a cold wind was howling outside. I couldn't take my febrile child out in that.

Then I heard someone open the entry door downstairs, a woman student from the school where my husband had studied and I taught. She had not been one of those who had offered her services to our household, so I had not asked her for any help. I emboldened myself and asked. Would she be able to come to our apartment for an hour or less, or could my child come up to hers? My neighbor was not warmed by the thought. She had two other people coming for a study group for an important exam. She had promised them this time. I explained my dilemma and assured her my daughter would just rest or read and not bother the students. My neighbor seemed irritated at the request and stuck to her plans with lofty finality. I felt I was groveling and had asked the unaskable—they were *my* children after all! As I remember, I was saved from hauling my sick child out into a developing snowstorm by the kindness of another day care parent who answered the phone when I called to say I would be late picking up my kids. He ended up driving his own and my kids through the perilously mounting snowdrifts in the crowded afternoon traffic. I was tremendously grateful to him but, at that point, felt one more weight of indebtedness piled on an already unsupportable load.

My experience was cushioned by the fact that this would all be over in a couple of months. Plus, I told myself, this was a lesson in learning to receive graciously as well as an opportunity to enter empathetically, albeit briefly, into a reality outside my own. But what of the many single parents who never see an end to the burden of being the only one to undertake the awesome task of parenting and providing full financial support? What weights of isolation and unwanted indebtedness do they shoulder year after year? How many initially helpful teams of friends do they see begin to avoid them or to dread their unspoken requests?

The second thing I learned in my brief life as a single parent was that the empty space left by the absent parent is not easily filled. I expected to miss my husband and I did. I did not expect the extent of my children's response to his departure. At home the baby did not seem appreciably different, but his behavior at our co-op day care was markedly altered. He began to forcefully reject the ministrations of his female caregiver and cling tenaciously to the fathers who came to be parent volunteers for the morning. Our middle girl, despite my attention and assurances that this was all temporary, became weepy and silent for a time. My eldest daughter simply rebelled against everything: getting up, going to bed, going out, coming home, getting dressed, getting undressed, and on and on.

It was not simply that they missed him but that *he* alone could adequately fill the gap he had left behind. This was stunningly clear to me the first week after his departure. I had, as I said, arranged for friends to drive my older daughter to her school in the mornings. This was the last thing I thought I had to worry about: one "chore" that my husband had always done was to be taken over by someone else. The first day she went cheerfully out the door with an upstairs neighbor. When she came home she slung her bookbag onto the table and looked me ruefully in the eye. "Is *that* the way it's going to be from now on?" she inquired.

"What was wrong?" I wanted to know. "Well," she said, eyes filling with tears, "when Daddy takes me I get to sit in the front seat and turn on the radio news and we discuss important things like politics and world hunger and stuff! Just him and me! The *other* guy gave the woman downstairs a ride and they carried on their own talk and I had to sit in the back seat! Like a package to be dropped off!"

How little I was aware of the unique presence that father and daughter shared in those twenty minutes before school each day. How little I had comprehended that this was not a "chore" that another could take over with ease.

The third lesson I learned during those months was double-edged. On the one hand, it was exhilarating to find out that I could do so much for myself. It was like going into a phone booth to make a call for help and discovering that I wore a wonder woman suit underneath my regular clothes. I also learned the price I had to pay for that thrilling discovery. During those months I lost ten pounds, became anemic, and got disgusted hearing people tell me a dozen times a day that I looked tired. My children also paid the price of sheer exhaustion. A dental exam given upon arriving at our new home revealed mouths full of cavities resulting from the depleted vigilance of a parent who could do no more by 9 P.M. than hope that everyone had taken care of their own toilet needs and brushed their own teeth.

My brief sojourn into single parent land likewise convinced me of the delicate nature of the intimate bonds that bind us in family. During the long periods when we didn't see each other, my husband and I spoke over the phone. But a marriage is not like a friendship which you can pick up after a lengthy interval. And it is very difficult to talk with much nuance over an electronic wire. Because a marriage involves the interpenetration of two lives on so many levels, it seems to require a great and continued proximity for a couple just to stay attuned to each other. And when discernments are being made and new situations adjusted to, people change. A spouse can only with difficulty be sensitive to the subtle shifts in perception and growth that occur in a partner if they are separated a great deal. From issues as mundane as deciding who will help the kids with homework to a Spirit-filled attentiveness to the questions "Who is God" and "How do I respond to God's call" that brood in the heart of a loved one, wife or husband need to be with one another so that all the levels of their shared life will remain aligned.

During those absences my children and I became an enclosed family unit. When my husband returned for the first visit we found, to our consternation, that he didn't fit in. We had choreographed behavioral and psychic dances into which he now plodded like an unwanted spectator. It took the majority of the visit to reconstellate our original family grouping—then we had to say goodbye again. The coming and going took more of a toll on our relationship then any previous difficulties we had struggled through while on the same turf. It made me recall the comment made by a graduate school professor of mine who traveled frequently. When he went away it always took the same length of time as the trip itself to "make up" with his family for being away. And his family was genuinely supportive of his occupational journeying.

It should not be surprising that the rate of marital attrition is very high among those whose work requires prolonged absence—the military, for instance. Being a parent and a spouse requires that you help to create a living community of care and attentiveness twenty-four hours a day. If you are frequently apart, you must nonetheless create that community. You must live as a single parent, an experience which is occasionally exhilarating, mainly overwhelming, frequently lonely and haunted by the reminder of "empty drawers."

Alone Yet Not Alone

Yet there is a beauty in the experience of parenting alone. You find yourself thrust to a remarkable degree upon the grace and love of God. Without the loving arms of a partner to embrace you, God's open-armed invitation takes on new urgency. Without the support of one more point of view, you find yourself uneasy about simple decisions and overwhelmed by the major problems that arise in the course of familied life. God as a forgiving presence, as gentle confidant, as the ultimate source and caregiver of your children, is available in a heightened way.

I do not want to suggest that the discovery of God's presence in the face of absence is an easy matter. It is, in fact, very hard. We are accustomed by nature and training to seek the face of a God whose loving touch is mediated through the persons and things we love. We also, rightly, identify the experience of the presence of God with all that is healing, whole, enhancing, and full of life. We are drawn to all that exudes those qualities and shy away from suffering, loneliness, and barrenness. This is a healthy instinct and I would question the motives of those who always oriented themselves toward pain and life-denying situations on their spiritual journey.

Yet, as an issue in the spirituality of family, the discovery and the experience of absence can be a rich soil for the seeds of spirit that we plant. We forget that we have faith in a God who not only creates us but a God who enters into *all* of our humanness. We cling to a God who encountered the most terrible of human suffering and who absorbed the fullness of evil that humankind can muster. Our God embraced all this so utterly that divine forgiveness and ultimately, the power of love which *is* God, triumphed. Life over death. Joy over sorrow.

Yet it was *through* the process of losing all that this came to be. I would never suggest that God *wills* our suffering, our divorces and the deaths of those we love. Nor would I ever counsel those in families where abuse or sorrow exists to "accept it with patience" or "to be Christlike." The mystery of our faith consists in the discovery that God is greater and larger and more sustaining than anything else, that God is with us when we are least able to recognize the divine presence.

What we feel when we open the empty drawers of our lives is the pain of absence where presence once was. The joyful discovery of the Christian is that even in emptiness, in the void, a constant and more joyful presence truly lives.

DEEPER
WITHIN

·6·

There are common parts of the home where everyone is welcome, where guests mingle with those who live there, where the dynamics of the family may be viewed by others. There are also private areas as well, places of intimate encounter, places not visited by the stranger and known only by those who inhabit the family home. Anyone who has visited people they do not know well will be familiar with the curious sense of hesitancy, or even trespassing, when they enter the intimate parts of the house, perhaps passing through the upstairs sleeping quarters to use the bathroom or going to the back of the house to retrieve a coat that has been laid in the master bedroom. Every part of the home says something about the people who live there. The inner parts speak in a hushed and private tone.

A light is flicked on in the search for the coat. A teenaged boy's room is filled with light. His world is floodlit for a moment—sports pennants, scattered school books, a ham radio dismantled on the floor, a bed unmade in the hurry of getting out of the house in time. Around the corner another room is illuminated—the clutter of a nursery, the bright primary colors of blocks and dollhouse furniture meet the eye, the nose detects the faint stale odor of milk and graham crackers, a well-fingered blanket hangs from the edge of the bed. One more darkened room is lit, the master bedroom emerges into view, perhaps spread with the muted colors of an executive's suite that coordinate with the dark stains of a hardwood bureau and chest of drawers. Perhaps this room is spattered all over with floral pastels that match the spring colors festooning the window casings in eyelet and flounce. Perhaps the bed is large and low to the ground, a heated waterbed casually draped in an Indian madras covering. Perhaps the bed is narrow and raised high, encased in the folds of a quilt that has been in the family for years. Perhaps the bed is crowded in on all sides by the paraphernalia of its inhabitants' lives: books, unopened correspondence, a home computer terminal, flower petals drying for potpourri. Perhaps the bed floats in a sea of serene space, blissfully aloof from its owners' possessions which all have discrete and appointed places in a closet or on a shelf.

Deep within the home lies the privacy and intimacy of the space where a man and a woman celebrate and ritualize their shared life. A couple's bedroom is a unique area in a home. A classic book on architecture and the timeless "patterns" of building speaks of the bedroom and the bed that it encloses in this way:

> the pattern, "couple's realm" . . . gives emphasis to the importance of the couple's private life together within a household. Within that couple's realm, the placing and nature of the bed is naturally the most important thing.
>
> The bed is the center of a couple's life together: the place where they can be together, talk, make love, sleep, sleep late, take care of each other during illness. But beds and bedrooms are not often made in ways which intensify their meaning and these experiences cannot take hold."[1]

This quote suggests that there is something unique about the psychic and spiritual dimensions of a man and woman's committed life together that requires nurture. Nurture is required in the form of architectural patterns that enhance and facilitate the human dynamics that are being lived out. The quote also suggests that other forms of nurture are required for the health and preservation of such dynamics. It takes much more than just love and good intent to realize a marriage. For a marriage is a complex intertwining of two lives on many levels—biological, social, economic, intellectual, and spiritual. All those levels must be attended to and continued to generate life-giving energy for the couple's shared experience.

The spiritual life of a marriage is as hardy and delicate as a dandelion that pushes its way against all odds through the cracks in the concrete sidewalk, yet can be crushed by a casual footfall. There certainly are a number of observable factors that can contribute to a couple's successful union: similar backgrounds, shared values and expectations about everything from finances to whose family we're going to spend the holidays with, growing up with healthy models of intimacy and parenting, a certain maturity and willingness to grow. The list could go on. These are part of the environment that nurtures a couple and are essential to its flowering. But these factors do not define the spiritual life of a marriage. The nurture and growth of the inner life of such a union require utmost seriousness, mingled with a sense of play and the capacity for surprise.

The bed symbolizes that reality.

Male and Female God Created Them

Love through intimacy is like the rain that softens the
endosperm of a seed so that it can germinate and grow.
Without intimacy love does not touch us and in turn we do
not grow. And it is growth that God is concerned about. For
God is like the good farmer who knows that if a plant (us)
is not growing, it will soon die. And in the death of a plant,
not only does the plant lose its life, but the farmer loses the
fruit of the plant that S/He had been counting on. So God,
like the farmer, does not want the life in us "plants" to die.
S/He wants us to continue to grow and that growth is
possible only when we are most deeply related to others.

> James Regan (farmer and lay student at a
> U.S. Catholic school of theology)

I first met my husband in late springtime. Spring on the California coast is the time of year when the habitual fog of early mornings has ceded to the insistent sun, the long afternoons lie indolently over stretches of green grass, and time breathes as gently as the wind in the blossoming fruit trees. Even today I see him leaning against the trunk of a plum tree on a square of lawn in the middle of a university quadrangle. He is in shorts and sandals with the straw brim of an insolently raked cowboy hat settled down so far over his eyes that his face is all auburn mustache and teeth—those teeth my mother named so well in a ladies' restroom where she and I found ourselves after I first introduced him to her. "Well," she breathed as I waited for her first reaction following their meeting, "he certainly has magnificent teeth!"

86

Whenever I have lost track of that boy-man in the midst of income tax returns, the scheduling of softball practice and dance classes, the continual hassle of everyone using the same bathroom, I think of him at that moment, frozen in time, beneath the plum tree, and I look in wonder and concern and gratitude at what he and I have become.

Not all families have as their nucleus a husband and wife. Some single-parent families have never had a couple at the helm. Others have seen the death of the intimate coupling that brought the family into being. While I do not wish to exclude these families from any of these reflections, still I cannot exclude from these pages a real, if limited, attempt to speak of marriage as a positive and graced part of family life. In fact, I would like to explore the marital bond in sacramental terms.[1]

Not all Christian communities include marriage in the official list of sacraments that are recognized as channels of God's grace. By *sacrament* I refer to a sign of some greater reality, a way that the invisible is made visible. In the Roman Catholic tradition marriage is considered a sacrament along with baptism, confirmation, Eucharist, penance, extreme unction, and holy orders. Its celebration is seen to deepen the union of the recipients with the Church as the body of Christ.

In other denominations marriage is not viewed in this light. Whether you consider marriage to be a Sacrament (big *S*) or not, I think the nature of marriage is to be sacramental (small *s*)—to be a way of life that in itself affords us the opportunity to see, to touch, and to live out of a more fundamental reality than the one we perceive on first glance.

Almost every couple is aware of this at one time or another. My impression is that most are not able to speak of their perceptions. God and God-things tend to be associated exclusively with the church building, with formal prayers or a set of beliefs, with a particular moral code and with an act of blessing that sit atop a basically secular relationship, like the white icing on a wedding cake that often gets scraped to the side of the plate because eating too much of its sickly sweetness is not appealing to most tastes.

Nonetheless, the deeper perception is generally there. For some couples this is quite explicit. A husband and wife need only recall a moment in the course of their shared life when they sensed that they were in the presence of a mystery greater than themselves: the announcement of the first pregnancy, an experience of great and shared vulnerability during intercourse, the joy of genuine reconciliation when there has been misunderstanding or estrangement, the birth or death of a child. The times will be as unique as the couples themselves.

These moments are simply heightened intimations of the mysterious reality that lies at the heart of the marital relationship. These moments are many in kind, but they reveal a twofold dynamic that operates in the spirituality of marriage—the dynamics of intimacy and otherness. It is through these two channels of the sacrament that we discover together the very nature of God's self-revelation.

Intimacy

The sixth-century pope, Gregory the Great, wrote of the Christian life as a pilgrimage of desire. On the road to our final homeland, he claimed, we pilgrim people experience God as presence and as absence. In our journey we do not walk alone. Rather like the disciples on the road to Emmaus (Luke 24:13–35), we walk together. We talk of something we do not completely understand—our desire to know and understand God's ways. We feel the "absence" of God. In the process we share our desire. Our hearts burn in concert as we speak of the things for which we most long. In that burning, that shared desire, we experience presence. For God in this life is touched chiefly in the relationships of mutual desire that join us in our most authentic selves to bring us home at last.

Desire is present in every human love. Desire is the vital force that propels us out of ourselves into the aura of that which we love. Inherent in our maleness and femaleness, our sexuality, is this element of desire. We desire to be one with another whose way of approaching things differs from yet is complementary to our own. We desire him or her physically, emotionally, intellectually, and spiritually. We want to become one. This desire, I think, has everything to do with our spiritual wholeness and our becoming recreated in the image and likeness of God.

Male and female God created them. In God's own image they were created. Our desire to be in union with a chosen person of the opposite sex is simultaneously a desire to be in union with what is most expressive of God's own life in us, God's wholeness. To become united, however, with a man or a woman or with God, we must cultivate an expansive capacity for intimacy.

To be intimate with another does not just mean to have sex, it means becoming vulnerable and transparent enough to allow another to touch us at the most intimate levels of our being. It means we must learn to trust and be trustworthy. It means we must be prepared to let a relationship change us. It means we must enter into a long and continual process of self-revelation, allowing the self-imposed barriers that protect us from each other to be scaled or broken down. We must become known and know another in a unique way.

The image from classic spiritual literature of which this growth in intimacy is most reminiscent is the image of nakedness. I think especially of St. Francis of Assisi and his startling embrace of nakedness as an inner disposition suited to union with God. Francis saw in Jesus, particularly the cross-hung Jesus, the Way that the human person must respond to the God who calls out to be known and loved. Jesus stripped naked of everything—possessions, power, friendship, comfort—this Jesus St. Francis sought to emulate in every detail of his life. Francis became a beggar, refusing not only to own property but to handle money. He went barefoot, slept on the ground, refused to acquire education or accept privileges which could become an impediment to his physical and spiritual nakedness. The point of it all was to empty himself utterly to make room for God.

Francis's life witnesses to a naked spiritual state of readiness and receptivity that is unhindered by the overbearing demands of self. His life speaks of a person transformed, willing to be changed from within and willing to respond to another with genuine love. Marriage is one vocation in which this personal transformation is facilitated by the very state of life itself. The nakedness of husband and wife together, which must occur on all levels of the person, is profoundly transformative. We may not always warm to the self-emptying to which marriage calls us, nor do many couples take the opportunity to really explore their shared nakedness as a rich ground out of which a compassionate and other-directed self can spring. But the opportunity is there. The art lies in discerning what in fact is authentic nakedness.

For nakedness is not nudity. The distinction is crucial, I think, for in our present American culture we see much nudity and little genuine nakedness modeled for us. Nudity is a state of self-consciousness that sees itself being seen. It is deliberately provocative and exercises considerable manipulative power; it is calculated to arouse a desired response in the viewer. The nude is the object seen, and the nude as well as the viewer is engaged in the process of seeing. Nudity thus erects boundaries between people because it objectifies the viewer and the viewed.

Nakedness, on the other hand, is not self-conscious at all. It is not concerned with appearance or effect but with relationships. It requires a transparency of person that seeks to dissolve the boundaries between self and others. In its powerlessness, true nakedness disarms the other and invites a naked response. Contrast the nudity of *Playboy* or pornographic literature with the innocent nakedness of a child or the heart-breaking vulnerability of the photos of naked concentration camp inmates. Contrast the responses they evoke and you see the point vividly illustrated.

True nakedness that leads to intimacy between people is a graced state of being. Yet our contemporary culture and our church do not encourage us to explore its possibilities. In a recent sociological study the special "habits" of the American heart have been described in a way which, it seems to me, helps us to look at ourselves in a new and insightful way.[2]

Americans, this study suggests, are not oriented toward relationships of interdependence but toward individualism. We look out for "Number One," we are preoccupied with "how to succeed," and we challenge our children to compete against each other for the goals of self-development. We perceive the individual as over and against others, rarely as an essential but interconnected part of a whole.

Leavened with a strong sense of civic duty, this individualism has its positive value. But divorced from any more communal ethic, our American penchant for individualism runs amuck. We tend to assess anything in our lives, including our relationships, on the basis of whether or not they continue to enhance individual achievement. Certainly, there is a healthy instinct that underlies such an impulse if it is motivated by a desire to counterbalance an oppressive communal ethic that squelches or submerges the individuals in the life of the whole. Americans seem to have swung to the reverse extreme pole. Individualism as a good in itself is often pursued to the exclusion of relational needs and responsibilities.

In the development of marital intimacy, the implications are many. This is a delicate question and as I proceed I think it will become clear that I am emphatically *not* espousing a sort of marital relationship centered on the concept of duty defined as surrender to the good of the marriage at all costs. But we are, as a people, not disposed to open ourselves to the profound risks of intimacy. We are not always prepared to slog through the painful processes of transformation with which the intimate encounter of married life challenges us.

On the flip side, I'm not sure our churches often offer us a viable alternative vision to straddle the "each-one-for-him/herself" model. They too often seem to espouse an oppressive "everyone deny their own individuality for the sake of the family" version of matrimony. I have heard too many stories of women who functioned for decades as codependents with their alcoholic husbands while tolerating unspeakable abuses in the name of "turning the other cheek" or "just loving the way Christ did," to feel that this "self-sacrifice" is anything but self- and other-destructive. And I have seen too many marriages arranged on the "he makes all the decisions and we just obey" model not to mourn the loss of moral judgment and true discipleship that could have belonged to the "shes" and the "kids" who have settled for an essentially vicarious faith existence. The discernment in a marriage that finds true nakedness between the pitfalls of overweening selfhood and self-denial is a delicate and exhilarating one.

Intimacy is a key issue here. Perhaps the best illustration of what I am getting at is provided by the story of a Catholic laywoman of about fifty-five who shared the story of two wedding anniversaries with me, her twentieth and thirtieth.

She began by saying that she and her husband had decided not to celebrate their twentieth year together because to do so would be a charade, masking tensions, disharmony, and mutual disappointment. To do so would simply be too painful. Yet their thirtieth anniversary was a virtual festival. The grown children came back to toast them, and the family's sense of joy and harmony reigned throughout the day. What had happened in the intervening years?

She and her husband started their life together with high expectations. Both were very devout Catholics, who, as was common in their generation, never questioned any of their faith's teachings. A first child was born nine months after the honeymoon. The daughter was welcomed joyfully and became the focus of their life. Soon afterward the woman became pregnant again, but this time she miscarried. There were several more miscarriages until another pregnancy was assured—twins were on the way! But this required that the woman take to her bed for nearly the entire length of the gestation. Her first child, then a toddler, was forced to spend most of her days penned in a small safeguarded area where her confined mother could see her. The mother spent heartbreaking hours listening to her child clamoring for attention, afraid to get up lest she lose the growing life inside her. There were no nearby family members or friends to assist her. After the birth of the twins she had multiple miscarriages and one more live birth before the frightening edict that another conception could well cost her her life. She and her husband were sternly advised by their parish priest to quit the marriage bed and lead chaste lives.

Then I heard the heartbreaking story of two people who cared for one another deeply, who had seen the fruition of their love flower around them, begin deliberately to crush all expressions of the intimacy that bound them together. Any tenderness, any shared vulnerability was felt to be out of the question, for it could arouse the desire to consummate their union once again. What had been a warm and life-giving sharing became cold and dead. The cancer of the coldness crept into other aspects of their relationship and into the heart of their family.

On their twentieth wedding anniversary when this couple realized they could not bear to publicly celebrate their marriage, they finally had the courage to sit down and reflect together on their shared life. All the hard questions were asked and they told each other what was in their hearts. Then they set out to repair, as much as possible, the torn fabric of the intimacy. It took ten years of arduous reconstruction to once again live together in emotional, spiritual, and intellectual as well as physical union with each other.

This Catholic woman's story was, strangely enough, *not* one told to advocate the use of birth control or sterilization. This was a story about how the delicate life of spirit in a marriage must be responsive first of all to the cultivation of true intimacy. This tale spoke clearly of the dangers of authority when power is exercised without attention to the actual lived experience of marriage.

Two decades later, this woman and her husband might have embraced the practice of natural family planning that allows them the freedom to both celebrate their bodily union yet choose not to conceive new life.[3] Or another couple, if they had freely chosen, might have found continued creativity in a chaste union. Or they might have entertained other options.

The point is, that they alone could know what was a life-giving choice for them. A married couple must pay special attention to the life of intimacy between them. Whatever decisions affect that intimacy—in any sphere, not just the reproductive—must take as a starting place the nurturance of the totality of their lives together. The decisions will be as unique as each couple, and the pair will no doubt come to several turning points during their marriage at which they will reevaluate the choices already made. In her own words, the point of this woman's story was that "authority needs to flow out of the particular experiences of intimacy." Not the other way around.

This is a delicate but important issue that the domestic church can well share with the wider Church. The statement that authority must flow out of intimacy and not the other way around refers to intimacy in its broadest relational terms. Family members know much about the sensitive and constantly flexible arts of parenting, mutuality, and effective cooperation. No one can tell you exactly how to keep healthy relationships alive, nor is this something that can be legislated or codified once and for all. Certainly, families need help in envisioning what their lives might be and help when their own resources fail. But, almost as much, they need to be empowered to trust the wisdom of their own experience and be emboldened to define, in the uniqueness of their given circumstances, what is life-giving and faith-enhancing. After all, "The Sabbath was made for humankind not humankind for the Sabbath."

Otherness

Intimacy and its realization is a central dynamic in the spirituality of marriage. However, it is not the only one. When a man and a woman "become one," they do not at the same time cease to remain two. There is a quality of "otherness" about the union of man and woman that is as much a part of the spirituality of marriage as is the quality of intimacy.

In a marriage that calls itself Christian, there must be an abiding sense of the equal dignity of both marriage partners. Our faith teaches that each of us is a daughter or a son of God and that the unalterable dignity of our being as such is to be celebrated. A shared recognition of this essential dignity must exist in a marriage. One partner does not own the other, one partner is not subject to the whim or will of the other. Responsive to one another, self-giving, yes. Dominated by or dominating, no.

When this shared sense of equal dignity pervades a marriage, it creates between the two people a curious, even awesome, sense that this wife or this husband is actually other. She or he is known and called by God in a unique way. While woman and man are bound in intimate union in innumerable ways, each is, at the heart of their relationship, utterly free. They *choose* to love one another. Each must also *choose* to speak boldly to the other if either begins to see the spirit of mutuality being betrayed.

Beyond this deepest meaning there are other realities that speak of otherness in a man/woman union. Most obviously, one is a man, the other is a woman. There is a certain complementarity yet distinctiveness of the sexes that is felt in any marriage. I do not mean that each has a preordained role that must be filled, but that men and women are not only biologically divergent but also tend to perceive and be-in-the-world in distinctive ways. Recent feminist research on the psychology of gender has suggested as much.[4] Again, I do not mean that either sex has to do certain things because of differences, but that we need to be sensitive enough to embrace the whole range of human experience.

In a Christian marriage (in which the "otherness" quality of maleness or femaleness should not become grounds for alienation or the subordination of one way of being to another) the intimate encounter with the other is potentially formative. In the preschool circles in which I have traveled there are a number of men who have taken either full- or part-time care of their young children. By their own admission, the acquisition of "maternal" qualities usually embodied by women (not, I think, simply because they are women but also because they have cultivated them through their experience as mothers) has been life-changing. The men felt more whole as people and discovered they had learned much about God's own maternal tenderness both toward their children and themselves.

I will never forget one day greeting my husband at the door after he had spent a long afternoon in the neighborhood tot-lot with our toddler and preschooler. This corner refuge from the busy streets of Cambridge was always full of moms or nannies and their popsicle-smeared charges in summer. It boasted a few benches, sandbox, swings, a slide, a handful of stalwart flowers, and a spigot that on hot days got turned on to become a welcome fountain for running under and splashing in. The playground was my destination for part of almost every sunny day. When my husband came in that afternoon after depositing the grimy socks and sandbox toys outside our door, he came over to me very excitedly, "I've seen a vision of the kingdom!" he announced. "If we all did that, all of us, fellow citizens, nations, within community, the kingdom would have come. There they all were, the stronger ones caring for those who were not strong, the endowed responding with care and attention to the needful ones. It was the simplest thing in the world. They were loving one another."

It is not simply in exchanging traditional sex roles that man and woman are enriched by the otherness but by just being together. There is a fullness to decisions made when both partners are involved. There is a complementarity to the way each man or woman comes to the central questions of daily living that, if given sway in a marriage, can produce a rich tapestry.

The sense of otherness in the spirituality of married life also comes from the fact that husband and wife are simply different personalities with diverse interests, backgrounds, and goals. While sometimes this can be frustrating, diversity can also change us and teach us something of God's ways. For it is easy to think that our own ways of being, doing, and understanding are normative for everyone.

To realize that someone else, especially someone you know and love well, prays differently and, in fact, experiences God in a way you do not, can be illuminating. Early in my husband's and my relationship, before we were married, I learned this lesson well. I was at a point in my own faith where God was felt as overwhelming forgiveness and mercy. This was such a powerful feeling that it seemed omniscient to me. Surely this was *the true* God who touched me in such healing and miraculous ways. I wanted my husband-to-be to sense something of what I knew. He, however, was at a very different place with God. At the time I judged that he had not yet "arrived" (an embarrassing admission to make, I must confess). He was wrestling with a Miltonic Father-God of judgment who had been pursuing him since his graduate school days in English literature. We carried on some impressively heated discussions about the nature of God. My not too veiled entreaties were designed to get him to see that *my* notion of God was true while his was essentially false. He, however, had the good sense to challenge me. One day there was an ultimatum I could not ignore. "If we are going to be together," he finally said one day, "then you will have to accept me where I am. Not with some notion that I'm going to come around. But *be* where I am. Stand with me where I am. If you can't do that, we can't go on." He meant it

Needless to say, I was sobered. Then followed one of the most eye-opening experiences I have ever undergone. I really heard him. Somehow I managed to abandon the idea that he would eventually see things my way. In fact, I genuinely entrusted him to God's own care. And I stepped, for a moment, inside his heart. I found there, not an experience of God that was to my taste, but instead an experience that had an inner logic and integrity all its own. I understood ("stood-under") his sense of God.

What I learned that day was twofold. I learned how to genuinely love this man who was to be my husband because I accepted his distinctive and mysterious relationship with God. I also learned that God is restricted in each of us by the specificity of our own experience. To respect God's way in the other is to learn a little more about God's self-revealing ways.

Intimacy and otherness: the tension of living joyously between these two dynamics constitutes the spiritual art of marriage. Love can only free husband and wife to the promised liberty of the children of God when the full dignity of each is recognized in partnership. They are called to mutuality: to exercise their judgment, offer their gifts and freely enter into the covenanted union of intimacy. They are called to be cocreators of the tiny Christian community formed by husband and wife and to participate in God's own creative activity through the conception, birth, and raising of children.

Mutual Discernment

Much is said in manuals on marriage counseling about the importance of effective communication to a successful relationship. Certainly this is true. But "communication" seems to me to be too narrow a term to connote what must go on in a Christian marriage. For "communication" involves two people. As Christians we must also be alive to the presence and directionality of God in our lives. The classic literature of prayer is imbued with this spirit. But most of that literature takes as its point of departure the relationship between the individual and his or her own God known in the depths of the heart.

Discernment refers to the art of learning to distinguish the "spirit" (through motivations, desires, actions, etc.) of God from "spirits" originating from other sources (either individual, collective, simply human or otherwise). This is an ongoing active process of listening and dialogue. Traditionally, one "listens" to the Spirit of God enunciated through Scripture, official church teaching, the wisdom of respected theologians, teachers and community members, the promptings of one's own conscience and heart. All these expressions of God's word are lovingly heard and sifted through to allow a pattern of meaning to emerge that speaks uniquely of God's "intent" for the individual at each moment of his or her life.

In a Christian marriage this process will go on for each of the partners. But it will go on, I think, *between* them as well. A man and woman who join their lives in such a radical way do not merely engage in individual discernment and then communicate with each other about what they have heard. They engage in what I would term "mutual discernment." This is a complex and delicate process of lovingly listening to the self, to the other, and to God known through all the traditional channels. For God is the third partner in the sacrament of matrimony. God's intention for each of the pair is the tender goad that prods each on to full potential. It is also the gentle urgency that acts within the shared life of the couple to encourage them to see and respond to all aspects of their lives as Christians. Mutual discernment involves not only how they will pray as a couple, or what church they will attend, but how they will make and use their money, what moral choices they will make in both "private" and "public" spheres, how they will be with others in the expanding circles of human community, how they will raise their children, and how they will live as citizens of the earth.

God meets a man and woman where each is. But God challenges all to grow beyond where they find themselves together. God's call is, first, to full human maturity but beckons far beyond that as well. God intends that all humans share in the *fullness* of life, a life animated by the divine. To know and to act upon the most God-centered longings of our hearts is the greatest of human adventures. The art of mutual discernment is at the center of a Christian marriage. All the tender and difficult listening and dialogue—with the "me," the "you," the "us," and the "greater than us"—is the challenge of a lifetime. To take on the challenge is to know what it means to be made in the image of God.

·7·

The custom in older homes was to place the cradle at the side of the parent's bed. Sometimes infants simply shared the big bed with their parents and graduated to more remotely located sleeping quarters only when the arrival of a younger sibling made it necessary. Often the adult bed contained a trundle bed beneath which could be pulled out for the use of the younger children in a family. Only older children slept beyond the confines of the parental room in a space of their own.

Today American children are more apt to sleep in a privately defined space early on in their lives, perhaps from the very beginning. Be this as it may, the older arrangement, which is still the norm in some homes, images for us the changing relationship of parent and child over the course of a family's life. Conceived in the bed shared by the woman and man, a child only gradually moves out of that intimate physical sphere.

The shared family bed, or the cradle at the bedside, expresses the physical, mental, emotional, and spiritual closeness of an infant with those from whom she or he came, especially the mother whose own body so recently was the child's cradle and rest. As a little girl or boy grows, the trundle bed, still in actuality a part of the bigger bed yet temporarily separable from it, serves as a nighttime nest. Like the growing child, cautiously defining his or her own sphere of identity, the trundle bed alternately turns away from and tucks back into the adult bed for storage.

The momentous move from family bed or bedroom to a room and a space of one's own mirrors the expanding world of the older child. Walls not only define a unique space no longer completely identified with mother and father; the walls of the child's room are the galleries on which hang the representations of the child's newly enlarged self. Music or film stars' portraits, athletic trophies, school memorabilia, all speak of the world occupied by the older child that is distinct from that in which father and mother live. Sometimes even the chaotic clutter of clothes, books, records, used dishes, and unmade bed serve to mark off this space from the serene neatness of the parental realms.

As with the psyche, so the spirit. From the intimate copenetration of woman and man comes a new life with its own deeply interconnected yet unique spirit. The child is destined to move from the confines of intimate parental space to spacious realms of its own, only to find itself capable of creating in turn a new intimate space where life again is born. In just this way each of us, conceived within the protection of God's own womb, is born to begin a special unrepeatable life, a growing up, away from the childhood bond, to the mystery of our adult dignity as cocreators with God.

The spirituality of parenting involves this curious dual knowing of ourselves: as figures of nurture and authority (who in some ways stand in the place of God for our own children) and as children profoundly dependent upon a greater nurture and authority than we alone can provide.

In the Circle
of a Mother's Arms

Our true mother ... feeds and fosters us, just as the great
supreme lovingness of motherhood wishes, and as the
natural need of childhood asks. Fair and sweet is our
heavenly Mother in the sight of our soul, precious and
lovely are the children of grace in the sight of our heavenly
Mother, with gentleness and meekness and all the lovely
virtues which belong to children by nature. For the child
does not naturally rely upon itself, naturally the child loves
the mother and either of them the other.

Julian of Norwich, *Showings*

Sometimes my eldest daughter and I collide. I, with the single-focused trajectory of a steel arrow, may be trying to herd children out the door or into bed. She, with the equally impressive dynamic of a monumental boulder, may have other plans. Sometimes we can manage to metamorphosize ourselves, becoming, say, two circus clowns who can laugh at their own quarrelsome antics, or two whitewater rapids whose currents merge into a tumultuous but one-directional stream. Other times, frustration, fatigue, and anger catch us in their nets. I become a mechanized earth mover, ruthlessly clearing all objects from my path. She becomes the obstacle to be unearthed. At times like these there are tears and sometimes the anguished cry, "I want Mommy!"

The first time she cried out in this way I remember shouting out in exasperation, "I'm here!" "No, you're not! You're not my

Mommy! I want my *real* Mommy!" she protested. "Is this a ploy, a power play?" I remember wondering. Is this an appeal to me to be what I cannot and do not want to be, some ever-smiling ideal mother like the ones depicted in baby lotion advertisements? Do I need to be firmer and more consistent in my discipline? Have I spoiled her? Is this a cry for help?

I have reflected for some time now on this curious exchange that we as mother and daughter from time to time used to enact. And while I continue to struggle to find the means by which she and I can more consistently be running water or circus clowns with one another, her cry, "I want my *real* Mommy!" has become food for prayer for me, taking me into a realm of self where my own capacity to mother in its most graced form lives and gives life.

What does it mean to be a *real* mother? Certainly it does not mean to imitate what our collective imagery has conjured up as the perfect mother, to become caught up in "mom-ism." The times in my life I have tried to play out this role, I have only ended up chagrined by my own limitations, angry at my children's lack of gratitude for my sacrifices and, most of all, filled with guilt. For the mothers who wax their linoleum in size six designer sportswear, preside over the family table (which is laid out with linen, offers home-baked bread, and is surrounded by cheerful children with impeccable table manners), lead the Cub Scout pack and the Little League cheering section, preside over classroom parties, are dressmakers for ballet recitals, hold down a little part-time (or full-time!) job on the side, and always smile, even when they have been awake for thirty-six straight hours tending a child with croup, do not exist.

I have come to see that my daughter's plea for her real mom is a religious intimation. It is a calling upon a *presence* that she sometimes feels coming through me—not when I am an "ideal" mom but when I am most deeply in touch with the source of unconditional love, when I begin to experience and to live out the reality that this love is indeed *with* us.

Holding Each Other

I have gradually come to learn more about this love-source, our God, through the lessons of motherhood.[1] It began for me in the nursing relationship that was the first matrix within which each of my children and I began our journey of mutual discovery. To nurse a child is to do so much more than simply to give nourishment. It is not only a means by which our species assures the physical survival of its young. To nurse a child is to enter into a complex, almost symbiotic, relationship with another human being. In nursing one learns two arts suited for the cultivation of the spiritual life: the art of attentiveness and the art of giving from one's own substance. Through these arts one becomes present to, one enfleshes, something of the graciousness of the "real mother." One enters the circle of the arms of our Creator, God.

The first six weeks or so of any nursing relationship are weeks of adjustment. Often there are mixed feelings, discomfort, and tedium. A woman and her infant are learning about one another. Each child nurses differently (there are snackers, voracious types, efficient ones, and lazy, sleepy babies). Each child and mother must gradually develop a pattern of responsiveness by which the mother knows when the baby is hungry, full, getting adequate nourishment, or experiencing some feeding difficulty. With some babies it is easy to tell. Others seem impenetrable in their cries. Whatever the particulars of the unique relationship, what is being developed during this time is the maternal art of attentiveness—that intuitive and attuned sensitivity to the internal rhythms and needs of someone outside oneself. One is learning the attitude of profound listening that characterizes the most contemplative of prayers. To learn attentiveness is a spiritual instruction. It is to perceive the self *in relationship*. It is to cultivate in the self the capacity for responsive action. For nursing requires not simply that one learn when to feed a child but how to feed it. A nursing mother often must learn how to relax and to position her suckler on the breast so that her milk will "let down." She must take care to nourish her own body, to get sufficient rest, to structure her other activities so that her milk supply is ample and so that she can be available to provide it.

Further, a woman who is nursing must learn attentiveness to the particular moment. There must be a certain unhurried quality of breastfeeding, a willingness to fully enter into the "what is" of the moment. A woman might daydream or read at times, but it is virtually impossible to nurse an infant in an attitude of impatience or of rushing on to the next scheduled event. Instead, attentiveness tends to focus a mother on the presence of her child, to enable her to perceive his or her unique face, hands, and body in a contemplative way, to see her baby as the mysterious gift of person that he or she truly is. Not that every feeding session becomes a time of such contemplative reflection—for there are hundreds of such sessions and their very routineness tends to dull perception of what might be experienced there. But always the possibility is present and the very nature of the nursing event, the way it enfleshes relationships, cultivates in a woman the art of attentiveness.

The art of attentiveness, of perceiving the self as part of a relationship, of "leaning into" that relationship with an attitude of listening, of cultivating the capacity for responsive action, of being in the present moment—this is an art that mirrors the art of prayer. At the same time, attentiveness is capable of becoming a spiritual dead end for a woman if it is not coupled with a strong sense of self-knowledge. Attentiveness can degenerate into simply living through someone else and it can lead to the parody of the person who is no person. But if attentiveness is cultivated as an art of self-giving, not of self-annihilation, it can yield blessed fruit.

A related spiritual art learned in nursing is the art of giving of one's own substance. Human milk is a substance obtained only at the cost of giving of one's own life energy. The nutrients stored in a woman's cells, the energy derived from the food she eats and the liquid she drinks, all are channeled into the production of milk. Every nursing mother knows how much fluid intake it requires to keep a hefty three-month-old fed and how tired she is at the end of the day spent in what sometimes seems like being "nothing but a milk machine."

Nursing draws upon one's deepest, most essential body resources. Moreover, it requires one to *be* there. A woman must offer herself to her child for however long it takes her baby to complete his or her meal. She must *be* food. She must allow herself, in the fullness of the love and delight she often feels, to be given over to another person. I have often thought that the communion meal that our Christian faith celebrates is best understood through reference to this art of giving learned in the nursing bond. As a people of faith we share bread and wine with one another. We enter into a ritual that bespeaks our true life as a community of mutual need and nourishment. Whatever theological distinctions our particular Christian denominations may articulate in regard to this meal, it is certainly always a sign to us that the living body of the faithful that proclaims Jesus as risen Lord *is* one body whose parts sustain life in the mysterious enactment of mutual need and mutual nourishment. We are called to be food and drink for one another, to give life, to share the substance of who we are, to have our deepest resources tapped so that the whole community can begin to realize something of the fullness of life that Jesus holds out as hope and *is*. What more powerful experience of this Christian life of ours is there than the nursing relationship of mother and child?

Being Held

As my eldest daughter reached preteen years her spoken demands for the appearance of her "real" mother decreased, but her need for me to embody those maternal qualities did not. It was at this life stage, when we were struggling with her incipient independent identity and readjusting who we were with each other, that my insights into who this "real" mother is became clear. Dis-

harmony between us threw me back upon prayer. There, struggling with my own sense of inadequacy, of limited resources, of
anger and pain, and reaching deep into the marrow of my prayer
to discover a source of life and hope that could exorcise my
demons of self-doubt, I discovered the warmth of the "real"
mother's embrace. Older children often do not want to be literally held because their sense of who they are does not allow for
such seeming lapses into the attitudes of early childhood. The
quality of parental holding must change, but "hold" them we
must, in hearts that expand to enfold their expanding selves. For
this, we need God.

It was a meditation on my own embrace of my children in its
most gracious form that led me into those wider loving arms. I
imagined my daughter, now fully grown, coming to me weary
with the burdens and experiments of life, coming to be held, to be
loved, to be nourished in the arms that had first given her some
intimation of the foundational goodness of life. In my own embrace I discovered that there was *nothing* that she could bring, no
experience, no pain, no excursion into the twisted labyrinth of
human frailty, that could separate her from the love I had for her.
This entering into the consciousness of the "real" mother brought
me into a realm of loving that was so expansive, so vast, that its
parameters could expand to contain all the pain, the failure, the
sinfulness that my daughter carried with her. The loving of the
gracious mother did not pretend that the pain did not exist. All
the weight of sadness and desolation that a parent feels for the
suffering of a child was felt and borne in that deep embrace.

The knowledge of my own capacity to embrace in this way
made me newly aware of the arms that open to me in this same
manner. God's arms are those of the "real" mother.

They are arms always open. They reach out for us, God's suck-
ling infants. We are the graced recipients of the nourishment we
need to sustain life through the tender ministrations of arms that
surround and support us, arms that tilt us gently to a food that
comes directly out of the substance and the deepest resources of

the maternal life itself. God feeds us like a nursing mother whose own flesh and blood are given to us for our life. God becomes bread and wine, blessed and broken for our eating and our drinking so that we in turn can be blessed and broken for each other.

I cannot claim to be a "real" mother most or even much of the time in my day-to-day interaction with my children. Unlike God, I am bound by severe personal limitations, often overwhelmed by the sheer effort of the task of childrearing, quixotic in my capacity to bring the fullness of who I might be to my children at any moment. But the "real" mother is there, not only as the matrix of love that embraces all created life, but woven into the fabric of my own experience, enfleshed in my own person and the persons of my children.

Moving Deeper into the Circle of the Mother's Arms

As my children grow and I have seen the art of child-rearing expand beyond the warm circle of my arms, I have begun to feel that my most pressing concern must be to move more deeply into the arms of the "real" mother. I suppose it is not accidental that it has been my own sense of limitations as a parent that has compelled me to this realization, for it is precisely the frightening experience of vulnerability, and lack that startles one out of the illusion of self-sufficiency and allows one to open to greater sources of strength and grace. We need to discover ourselves as children to discover our need for loving arms.

It is only recently that I have begun to have any real intimation of what it might mean to be a child of God. Certainly there are many ways of understanding this idea that is central to our Christian faith. For many years it was an image of my eldest at about one year of age that spoke to me of a quality of childhood that was also a capacity one would want to cultivate in relation to God. When we lived in California, I used to go for about a two-mile-long jog every morning just before my husband left for work. I would leave him and my toddler daughter busily engaged in washing the breakfast dishes. Soon, though, she would begin to miss her mom, and her daddy would pack up his things for work and carry her out to the end of the driveway to wait for my reappearance. As I rounded the corner of our block, I would see the two of them searching anxiously in my direction for the first sign of me. When she saw me, my daughter would squeal, scramble down from her daddy's arms, and begin to run toward me. Her running was utterly wholehearted and unselfconscious. She flew, breathless, into the open arms of the person she loved so much. Never mind that there were cracks in the sidewalk, that her shoelace might be untied, that her running steps were not yet sure enough to prevent a fall. She ran with the joy of pure love compelling her. I, on the other hand, was very aware of all the possible obstacles between us and our open-armed embrace. Yet I loved the abandon of her running, loved it and wanted to live that way, wanted to fling myself unguardedly into the arms of the God that creates and sustains our lives.

More recently, I have come to appreciate other qualities of childhood that we can claim as qualities that dispose us to go to God. In experiencing God as source of welcome and nurture, I have come to a new awareness of the heart of the child that seeks sustenance and rest near the heart of God. My imaginative meditation on my grown and world-weary daughter's return to me has prompted reflection not only on the nature of divine love but on the nature of human response to that love. The meditation is, of course, a variant of the story of the prodigal son, and like the errant boy my daughter returned to seek the shelter of home only after hitting bottom, after coming to the end not merely of physical but of personal and spiritual resources. In the Lucan narrative the son is reduced to tending pigs, animals considered unclean in the Jewish tradition, thus rendering himself a true outcast, an untouchable. It was only when he had reached that point, when he recognized his own terrible needfulness, that he discovered his need for his father's welcome embrace.

It is hard for any of us truly to accept our own vulnerability and insufficiency—both for each other and for God. Parents, it seems to me, are especially prone to harbor illusions of self-sufficiency. We who care for the young, who are called to be providers, shelterers, healers, teachers, and question-answerers for our children easily forget our own neediness. We forget that we too are children whose hearts must be open, trusting, and in need of God's deep embrace where all joy, all suffering is felt and borne. We must discover our true childhood so that we can return home, seeking those arms.

It is an art—a profoundly spiritual art—to learn to "lean into" or live consciously one's own need for God and others. Part of that art involves discernment of the seeming "needfulness" that is rooted not in love of God but in self-deprecation. Deep within the divine embrace the self is always recognized as infinitely precious, worthy of dignity and respect. One discovers one's essential goodness and the graced quality of one's life. When lack of self-worth, experiencing oneself as rightfully a victim, the absence of healthy self-love are detected, it is time to come closer into the aura of love that God projects. It is time to lean against God's heart to feel the gentle reminders that each of us is a gift, each created for the fullness of human dignity. In that embrace one discovers true needfulness and vulnerability, the heart of the beloved child that rests in loving arms and finds there its peaceful home.

Jesus in the Sermon on the Mount paints for us a portrait of the heart of the child who knows itself as blessed because it has experienced its own very lack as an opportunity to know and be known by God. The Beatitudes speak of blessedness. Those who experience their own poverty, weakness, mourning, and hunger are not blessed simply because someday all pain and suffering will be alleviated, but because their very neediness creates in them a heart that has room in it. Such hearts open out to others and to God. Such hearts are the very antithesis of those hearts filled with themselves, armored in power, intact in their own invulnerability which shuts them off from loving relationship with God and their fellow creatures.

To move more deeply into the circle of God's arms involves a radical entry into one's own vulnerability and need. The heart of the child with arms outstretched is a heart that knows both its own belovedness and its dependence upon those loving arms. It is also a heart that is open to all relationships, that, through experiencing its own childhood, knows the child in other hearts. It knows the hurt, the mourning, the poverty of all human hearts and seeks to be in communion with that state of blessed childhood in all God's people.

The prodigal child returning home has come to the end of all resources. She or he comes home not only to find the welcome and the nurture of the mother's embrace but comes home to find that human needfulness is deeply blessed. She or he discovers the richness of being poor in spirit, the intrinsic exultation in lowliness, the comfort in mourning, the fullness of hungering, the strength in mercy. The child feels itself nestled within the mother's arms and finds there, in that expansive love, that all the children are welcome, all the children are invited, through the open vessels of their hearts, to come into those arms and experience themselves as brothers and sisters nurtured by the same loving care.

·8·

In the corner of the bedroom is a well-worn rocking chair. The padded seat cover is faded and pressed flat from constant wear. The chair's arms are scratched. The rockers, too, show the marks of the many years of their backward and forward motion. The chair seems almost shaped, imprinted with the body it has supported for so long. This is woman's space.

I write of woman's space in the context of these essays on family spirituality for several reasons. First, for better or worse, woman and home have long been identified. Her voice, rarely heard, has been relegated to the cultural silence of the domestic sphere. Even when women have had a public voice—historically in the monastic communities of Europe and, more recently, in the various fields opening up to women—in these contexts women do not necessarily articulate the experience of *being* female. Yes, they may inadvertently speak in a "different voice" than male counterparts. But in the monastic culture or in the business and professional worlds, they rarely are called upon to speak on the experience of being female. This experience is sung mainly in literature. And it is to literature that investigators have tended to look in order to delve within the depths of the female spirit. But for the most part the available literature is neither overtly Christian nor concerned primarily with family.[1]

Within the home and within the tightly knit fabric of family relationships much of woman's spirituality comes into being. And much of that spirituality is deeply rooted in the body. In contradistinction to our Christian heritage that has been shaped by men's perceptions and has drunk deep of philosophical springs that often make a sharp distinction between body and spirit, the experience of woman in family cannot separate

113

the two. Woman's attention is given much of the time, at least subliminally, to the experience of being held and entered, to the cyclical wetness and dryness of fertility and infertility, to the flow and cessation of menstruation, to the profound body-changes of pregnancy, to the fluids of lactation, to the carrying, washing, feeding, and caressing of bodies, to the physical sensations of menopause. To pray a family woman's prayer is to celebrate, suffer, and grieve out of the miracle of the female body. It is to pray the whole person, body and spirit entwined. It is to pray with the rhythms of all created life.

Wreathed in Flesh and Warm

> A shape, like folded light,
> Embodied air,
> yet wreathed in flesh and warm;
> All that of Heaven is feminine and fair,
> Molded in visible form.
> She stood, the Lady Shekinah of earth,
> A chancel for the sky,
> Where woke, to breath and beauty,
> God's own birth,
> For men to see him by.
>
> Robert Stephen Hawker,
> *Aisha Shekinah*

It is unlike most other kinds of waiting. Certainly it is not like waiting for other anticipated events, even momentous ones: a long-awaited letter from a friend, a wedding day, a coveted job opportunity, the end of a painful illness. There is a quality, a texture to the waiting we do during pregnancy that is one only with the waiting we do for God.

That pregnancy and the entry of divine life into the world are inextricably related is, of course, at the heart of the Christian message. God became human in the person of Jesus through the person of Mary, through this woman's willingness to open herself, soul and body, to the divine seed that soon would flower for the redemption of the world. It was Mary's assent to the angel's startling announcement that ushered in a new age. It was in her pregnant womb that heaven and earth were so lovingly intermingled, through the waiting experienced in her flesh and blood that God was made to walk with humankind.

The majestic and cosmic implications of this unique pregnancy may fill us with an awe that separates us from intimate identification with what went on there. Yet there is a more personal dimension to that one creative event that does speak directly to each of us. Like the simple young woman in Nazareth, we may be surprised, at any time, by the intuition that we too are chosen. We are hailed to receive into ourselves the seed that God wishes to plant there. We say yes and the life of God begins its course of gestation in us. We become the ground out of which the incarnate God flowers in the world.

Mary's one unrepeatable pregnancy speaks to us of the life of the spirit growing within. This much we know. This much has been commented upon by Christian exegetes for centuries. But it is also true that each of our own pregnancies can speak to us of the direction of the divine wind moving in our world. For, if we are to take this incarnate God we worship seriously, we must come to learn that the wisdom of the created world, the wisdom of the body, is also the wisdom of the soul. There is grace at work in our blood and bones. There is divinity awaiting entry into human history at the threshold of our own hearts' doors.

Pregnancy is at the core of the Christian message. And so to gaze long and thoughtfully at the experience of pregnancy, especially as it is a process of waiting, is to learn something of the waiting we do for God, who breathes and moves in us, longing to be born. Perhaps being pregnant is so common an experience, so unconsciously connected to the self-identity of most women, that it may seem strange to look there for intimations of God's working in our hearts and in the world. Yet our Christian faith does not celebrate the reign of a disembodied Deity but a God who is with us, a God whose presence here on earth, to use the phrase struck by poet Robert Stephen Hawker in his poem *Aisha Shekinah,* is "wreathed in flesh and warm."[1]

Pregnancy is a time of waiting. It is, like the contemplative practice of the presence of God, a waiting that is also a "listening," a leaning inward toward the new life that is budding in the darkest center of one's being. I remember all three of my pregnancies as times of energy turned inwards, of what might have seemed a certain abstractedness or intimate preoccupation. In part this was simply a response to the biological fact that the creation of another person calls upon one's body to use all its available resources. Little energy is left over for outwardly directed activities. But the leaning inward of pregnancy takes place on another level, too, I would say. There is an attentiveness to the presence of another, a sensitivity to the cohabitation in time and space that is occurring within the deepest recesses of one's being. The other's presence is experienced in many different ways, which we shall explore; but there is an overarching sense of being in a different state throughout pregnancy. It is a sense of not being quite who you thought you were before. And the who you are coming to be has much to do with the life that is hidden inside.

Surrounding that unrevealed presence with one's questioning is part of the process of waiting. I am reminded of a statement made by a Trappist novice master I once met who, when asked about a life lived in Christian authenticity, responded that to be a Christian was not to know the answers but to begin to live in the part of the self where the question is born. He was, of course, not speaking about doubt concerning particular articles of faith but about a state of being. He was speaking of an attitude of listening, of awareness of presence, of an openness to mystery. A pregnant woman's questions encircling the seed inside her may come from many levels. They may involve wondering about the future child's sex, her own mothering capacities, its future rearing. But more deeply, the inarticulate questioning of pregnancy, that being present to the awesome and life-changing fact of the reality of new life, is like the age-old contemplative practice of the presence of God.

The consensus of many years of Christian prayer is that there *is* a presence into which we may enter. A presence that is unfailingly there. One of the most remarkable things about being pregnant, I remember, was the lived realization that, when one is pregnant, one is *always* pregnant. You wake up in the morning, move through the day, work, play, eat, love, and sleep pregnant. You cannot put it aside, take a vacation from it, and come back to it later. I am reminded of the story of Jonah and the intuition dramatized there that no matter where one runs, one cannot run away from God. For God is in the midst of us, in the very fabric of our lives. We can—Jonah-like—try to run away. We can fail, through the intentional or unintentional obstruction of our vision, to see the fact of the presence that is there. But it will pursue us and it will teach us its wisdom and direct us in its ways. Being pregnant, you are always pregnant. That fact pursues you and comes to inform everything you do.

Pregnancy is a contemplative time, a waiting like the waiting we do for God. In that waiting there are discernible rhythms which correspond to what I believe are two interrelated but distinctive processes. First, there is the rhythm of unfolding. To respond to this rhythm is to stay close to the hidden questioning going on within, listening to the answers that are not answers but that lead one deeper into the place of questioning. To be part of this rhythm of unfolding during pregnancy is to move quietly and inarticulately into the inward presence of another human person, to contemplate their personhood, to see their being through the eyes of God.

Waiting has yet another rhythm. This is the rhythm of the duration of the process, a journey which has a beginning, middle, and end. In each of our lives, God is gestated and born over and over again. And each time there is a birthing, there has been a journeying process, an inner pilgrimage with a map all its own. Waiting during these journeys has many qualities, each of which corresponds to the segment of road on which we find ourselves at any given time. Not only is the waiting different at the start of a journey than at the end, but the identity of the pilgrim—the way we view ourselves and what we are about—changes along with the shifting landscapes. This self-identity, which, I believe, is linked to the unfolding quality of the waiting, occurs simultaneously with the changing process of the journey itself.

How different the identity of a pregnant woman in the first trimester of her pregnancy from the identity of a woman close to term—both for herself and for those around her. During the first few months a pregnancy may hardly reveal its full potential. It may seem as though what is happening at this point of the process is little related to what the end result will be. That early time may yield very few symptoms, perplexing the woman and making her want somehow to have confirmation of the fact of the life growing in her. How many women I have heard say (especially in their first pregnancy) that they couldn't wait "to show," to feel and look "really" pregnant. Or the first months may be a time of fatigue or debilitating nausea. It may hardly feel full of life or in communion with the creative capacities of God's world.

The first signs of presence are often unclear. There is during this time a longing for clarity, for confirmation, for a more embodied knowledge of what is within you. Yet there is no way to hurry the process, no easy remedy for discomfort or the lack of sign. In gestation waiting must be embraced. For there is nothing to do but wait. And the waiting of this early phase is, again, unlike most other waiting, for you are not waiting for the presence to go away but to show itself differently, to blossom into the visible statement of a swollen belly or to yield to the radiant surge of energy and the healthy glow of pinkened cheeks.

Yet in that invisible and sometimes tedious waiting, when your whole body does not yet proclaim who you are and what you are carrying, when the secret is hidden within the recesses of your inner space, when you alone, or only a few persons close to you, know "the truth"—in that waiting there is an emergence of a new sort of question. Perhaps in many women it is not a question consciously asked. In some it is. The question is, "Who am I now that this surprising presence lives within me?" I think the answer is learned only over the long history of a lifetime, but its germ is present especially in the waiting of the early months. There is something, someone else who lives in me, to whom I am intimately linked. That someone, that intimacy, makes me someone different than I was before.

I have heard women in this first waiting time say, "I can't believe I'm actually going to have a baby, my own!" It is as if somehow the full reality of what is hinted at in the simple fact of being "barely pregnant" is glimpsed. Something very important is underway, and the present perception of it both lacks understanding yet grasps the momentous import of what is coming to be.

The contemporary phrase, descriptive of the state of God's kingdom in the world—"already but not yet"—is wondrously enfleshed in the waiting of the first months of pregnant life. So, too, it is in that other gestation of the Spirit within each of us. We have opened ourselves to the seed of God's own life, perhaps through prayer or through the shock of a crisis or the influence of someone else. Now we wait, barely conscious that what is planted inside can and will bear fruit.

Our waiting on God is not simply passive, however; it is active. God's life requires nurturing and attentive care for it to come to birth through us. The wisdom of our pregnant bodies tells us as much. I will never forget my amazement, the first time I was pregnant, at the fact that the gestation taking place asked so much of me. It was not only that I had to alter my accustomed routine but also that this emerging life became the focus of my whole person. It caught me up totally. My hormonal system shifted, my blood volume increased, the texture of my skin began to change, my gums became inflamed. I had a terrible craving for protein foods and an unavoidable need for long, deep periods of sleep. That little life within had taken control over the whole of myself, and its needs suddenly took priority over many otherwise necessary and interesting priorities.

I remember being amazed at the extent to which all this took place outside of my conscious control, at how much this female rite of passage was a larger and more primal process of which I was only one small part. That knowledge, that being caught up in the matrix of creation itself, deepened my sense of question. "Who am I?" I asked. "How am I different now that I see myself from the perspective of this primal human/divine process that is gestation and, ultimately, birth?"

This sense of being caught up with the whole self, of being asked actively to nurture what is growing within, is a characteristic of the spiritual life as well. We do not simply assent to God's presence; we *incarnate* it. It comes to be through the longing of our hearts and the labors of our bodies. It comes at the expense of the very life that courses through our veins.

God is born in time. Yet at the meeting of divine and human, time is also timeless. It is this quality of waiting that, for me, characterized the second phase of my pregnancies. The unseen was by this time beginning to be seen, the sense of "just being sick" was giving way to renewed energy and health. And the miracle of what was happening was slowly beginning to dawn on me. The restless perplexity of the first trimester was gone, but I had not yet entered the later period when the sense of immanence was heightened. I was just waiting.

Visibly pregnant with that gently rounded contour that is still manageable and not yet heavy with the ripeness of the last months, I experienced the eternal quality of the life of God within. It was as though this secret within me, to which my continual if unfocused attention was drawn by its very incarnateness, was leading me to a dark and hidden realm of existence. Here I was, at the first moment of creation, at the imperceptible moment when what had been nothing was suddenly something, when—at God's bidding—the unstirred was stirred. I was in the realm of God's own mysterious life force where beginning and ending become fused in a totality of meaning, where out of no time a finite human life erupted into the stream of history and began its pilgrimage.

Simply being during this time was miraculous, especially during my first pregnancy when I had the leisure (because I did not have other small children) to reflect on the experience and to respond to the pressing need for rest and proper nourishment. It was contemplative waiting during these months, a dawning awareness of the still center within which the human person opens out onto the divine life. Being was rich and infused with stillness, informing my continuing question, "Who am I now?" I began to have a sense of what is meant when we who are parents are referred to as cocreators with God.

Yet, the sense of the timelessness of the waiting does not characterize all of a pregnancy. The waiting can be very hard. In part, this is because the waiting is *for* something, not simply an end in itself. What is hidden wants to come to light. What is gestating wants to be born. And we press forward in anticipation, longing to know, to touch, to hold, to see, to name. In the classic spirituality of Ignatius Loyola this longing—the desire of the human heart—is seen as both a prerequisite for and the central dynamic of the life in God. In Ignatius's view it is our deepest desires that point us toward the ultimate object of our longings—toward God and the fulfillment of our hearts. There is, then, in the waiting upon God an element of restlessness, an intuition of incompletion which goads us to question, to discern. The waiting is not passive but catches us up in its inner dynamism. So too, a waiting pregnant woman aches to finally hold her child in her arms and call it by name. Her desire is for the issue of the vital process occurring within.

Waiting can be hard for another reason. The pregnancy may be fraught with discomfort and inconvenience; it may be attended by anxiety of many kinds; it may be dangerous, life-threatening to either the woman or the child. This is especially true of the last trimester when, even under the best of circumstances, the strength and size of the developing life within impinges on a woman's being in a way that is often difficult. Backaches, varicose veins, swollen ankles, high blood pressure, sleep difficulties, fears about the health of the child, anxiety about the impending birth, uncertainty about the community, the world into which this child comes—all these may make the waiting hard.

The fears, the pains are real. They are part of the stuff of the miraculous waiting. They speak to us, they embody for us the truth that there is no new life without a dying, no effortless way to be part of the creative process operative in this, our God's world. We do not give life without giving of our own lives. So, too, we do not bring God's spirit to birth without suffering, without giving out of the very substance of who we are. This hardness of the waiting, in both spiritual and physical pregnancy, speaks to us of another face of the incarnate divine life that we celebrate. There is a darkness to our God, a suffering and dying visage, that we sometimes choose to ignore. It is not easy to ignore the pains of physical pregnancy. But we do recoil from spiritual darkness both in ourselves and as it is manifest in our world.

Yet our bodies tell us, as do the symbols of our Christian faith, that suffering with the pain, being part of it, is what we must do. For in that pain, that shameful vision of our dying God, we begin to experience the answer to our most urgent human questions. We begin to understand communion, compassion, and participatory love. We begin to enter into the life that God intended for us, a life in which we live out the profound interconnectedness of us all. This life is symbolized for us in our Paschal Lord. It is also embodied in a woman's flesh.

What pregnant woman does not have a body-knowledge, perhaps only unconsciously appreciated, of the intimate connectedness of all life? What pregnant woman does not have some sense of the blood that invisibly flows between us, a torrent whose waters course unchecked through our own veins, through the veins of our children and our children's children, whose waters came to us through our own mother's swollen body?

A pregnant woman is not simply a self, a discrete entity maneuvering deftly among other discrete selves. She is bound, at the most intimate center of her being, to another being. She is linked, blended by the tissues of her body, to another life. Through the hardness of the waiting of pregnancy—a hardness that exists because of the shared quality of being in the waiting—she knows the sweet yet costly truth of the interconnectedness of all life.

The question evolving through the process of pregnancy— "Who am I?"—comes to be answered this way: "I am a somebody whose life is intimately and for all times connected to another life, and through that life, to all other lives." I think of that curious and touching communion of pregnant women I discovered with great surprise the first time I was pregnant. The body wisdom I discovered there identified me with all those named and nameless women who have for nine months been at the center of creation, the center of the web of life. I was initiated, too, by my physical coexistence with another person, into the communion of blood and water that binds all life together. And I became intimate with the timeless moment at which the Creator and the created meet, conscious of the still point inside the life that I am where new life is born.

The wisdom of the body is the wisdom of the soul. Divine life is encoded in human flesh. We wait for God's life to grow in us, to enter the world. The waiting can be hard. We can be spent in the process. The spending can impinge upon us in ways we could never have imagined. It may feel as though the marrow of our bones is being sucked out, as though we must die before God can be born through us. But the mystery we live is that our suffering is also a new birth. There is really one greater and more generous life of which we are one part. Our being born into it, our allowing it to come through us, is part of the creative and redemptive process of our God.

Pregnancy is at the core of the Christian message. We are pregnant. We are the place of waiting, the place of the question, of the advent. We are the womb through whose pulsing life God is born.

·9·

Most of the inner parts of the home, while they are not immediately accessible to the visitor, are visible if one is invited or happens into the home's intimate spaces. But on occasion there are locked doors, would-be entryways whose impassibility makes us aware that there is something within the life of the family that is hidden or barred from view.

The sad statistics on family violence in contemporary America make us aware that many such locked doors hold behind them the secret pain that many families endure. Often addictive or abusive patterns are passed down from generation to generation, the "sins of the fathers" being visited on the children. Family members live with these terrible secrets in fear, afraid to disclose the truth to public scrutiny, misbegottenly loyal to loved ones, maybe convinced that it is really "all their own fault," feeling helpless to act or fearful that speaking out would result in the withdrawal of love or the infliction of physical and emotional harm.

Locked doors within a home speak of the darkness of the room beyond, the cold and haunted darkness whose specter, though avoided, gradually permeates all the home's other rooms. It makes of the intimate warmth of bedrooms a mocking fire and the comfortable hospitality of the common rooms a place of strained reserve. It makes home a place in which, as one woman recalled, "I could never sit with my back to any door for fear of what at any moment might come through."

There are many authorities on and therapeutic approaches to the phenomena of family violence that can speak to its pathology and treatment more effectively than I can. But I do know this. Those doors must be unlocked and the darkness that they hide exposed to the full light before any healing can take place.

And light is already present, even in the impenetrable darkness, in some way or the other. There is nothing outside of God, nothing so seemingly antithetical to God's Spirit, that is not in fact within the circle of compassionate divine arms.

Transfiguration

I am the light of the world;
anyone who follows me will not be walking
in the dark but will have the light of life.

John 8:12

One of the Eastern Orthodox church fathers wrote an illuminating commentary on the gospel account of the Transfiguration. The usual treatments of that event, in which Jesus with several of his disciples is recorded as going up to a mountain to pray, being transfigured with light, and appearing for a time in the company of the prophets Moses and Elijah, emphasize the change that occurred in Jesus himself. His messianic identity is understood to be revealed. But Eastern Orthodox tradition points to the change, not in Jesus, but in the perception of the disciples as the key occurrence at the Transfiguration. They saw, the Eastern father explains, what was there all along but which until then the disciples were unable to perceive—the divine light that exists (through Christ) at the core of created reality.

At the center of the Eastern Christian mystical tradition is the doctrine of deification or becoming like God. Fallen humankind, that branch of our collective heritage assumes, was created in the divine image and through the Incarnation of Christ made capable not only of cooperating in the restoration of that image but of experiencing the divine nature within. The metaphor used to describe this process of deification is the image of light. The divine nature within the human person is to God's essential nature as rays of sunlight are to the sun itself, participating in but not identical with their source. God, uncreated light, cannot be seen in true essence. Nonetheless, God is made known to and in humanity through visible light or energies. Through ascetic practice and disciplines of prayer, the Christian is made transparent, and those divine energies begin to be manifested as visible light in his or her own body. The disciples present with Jesus on the day of the Transfiguration experienced a vision of the light that is the uncreated divine nature present in creation.

Moving into the Light

There is no way to take up the topic of violence within family life without hesitating. Much is written about the topic these days, and readers are referred to more competent sources than this book when dealing with the complexities of issues involved.[1] Still a few words are called for because a spirituality that ignores the dark side of human experience is a false one. Such a spirituality does not address people in the fullness of their experience or represent the breadth of the gospel message which proclaims a God whose own compassion reaches into and redeems through what is darkest and most painful in human life.

A play of images of light and dark, sun and shadow is called for here. Always I would like to keep in the background those perplexed disciples, surprised in wonder at the brilliance of the transfigured light they beheld.

First, the dark. Darkness or secrecy is to be avoided when dealing with abuse or addiction in family systems. The truth must come into light. Naming abuse, crying out against betrayal, confronting abusers, refusing to be victimized are essential. There can be no true Christian love if such things are allowed to exist in the name of "self-sacrifice," or "turning the other cheek" or "wives are subject to their husbands." My impression is that there has been a tendency in many of the Christian churches, when approaching family violence, to sweep outrage under the rug in the name of preserving family unity. What is at stake here is clarifying an issue in traditional Christian teaching.

There has long been an accent in Christian teaching that promotes self-denial. This is fine as long as the self-denial comes from an overflow of gratitude and genuine love, and is, in fact, self-gift. This is also fine (and definitely salutary) if self-denial is practiced by a person with a developed (even overweaning) sense of self. If a person has no healthy "self" to deny, then there can be no true giving. This teaching is particularly tricky for women or minorities or people of marginalized status, for culturally they have not always had the opportunity to develop a sense of self beyond secret self-loathing or self-deprecation. For these persons to "deny self" is to further perpetrate cycles of domination and subordination that cannot be considered Christian in any way. In fact, healthy self-love grounded in a sense of being beloved by God is, from a pastoral perspective, perhaps what is most needed by contemporary Christians today.

So sometimes being self-assertive in confronting those perpetrating violence is a thoroughly Christian stance to take. For there is sin in being complicit or codependent in actions or patterns of relationship that hurt and scar the God-given dignity of each human being. Abuse needs to be brought into the light. Physical or psychic violence festers and grows in secrecy and darkness, clouding the radiant image of God in humankind.

Presence of the Light

There is another facet of the prism of family violence: changing patterns of light and dark that emerge as we turn it around. Often in the classroom I am asked by persons involved in ministry to families in crisis, "What can I do for them?" They are not asking me about techniques of family therapy or for referrals to social agencies that can intervene to stop the cycles of destruction in which families find themselves caught. They are asking the deeper pastoral and even personal question, "How can I adequately respond to the depth of the suffering that I experience in the families among whom I minister?"

Again, images of light and dark come into play. What we really have to offer others, whether we are trained social workers, hospital chaplains, specialists in family systems therapy, or simply motivated by Christian charity, is our presence. To genuinely be present to, to suffer with another is a mysterious and transforming experience for all involved. To stand in this relationship to another or others requires that we do not know all the answers. We are not there as "fix-it people" but rather to use whatever skills we have to allow the intrinsic light in the perceived darkness to shine through. Our authentic presence, to be healing in any way, must take us into the presence of our own darkness. To minister to families in crisis, we must discover in ourselves the seeds of violence, cruelty, and neglect that we see in flower around us. We must know both the height and the depth of the human condition and embrace it with compassion. Only then can we be genuinely and transformatively present.

Often our being present will take us deeply into the enigma of theodicy. We will simply stand mute before the darkness and add our cries to the cries of those afflicted, calling out our questions to a seemingly deaf universe.

Even in this dark experience of presence there is the light of Christ. For darkness shared is one of the most profound, if least articulated, of human exchanges. To be present to families in this way is to bring to them the experience of companionship in their dark night.

Yet sometimes presence, especially as a recognition of one's own dark capabilities, provides the catalyst that pulls back the heavy coverings which prevent another from sharing in the light. I will never forget a lesson I learned at a workshop on Nonviolent Approaches to Resolving Conflict sponsored by Pax Christi, the Catholic peace organization. We were role-playing different conflict situations, being asked to alternately play the part of those involved in conflict or those intervening to defuse the tension.

One was a mundane scenario: a woman in a grocery store is aggravated beyond restraint by the antics of her child and verbally and even physically begins abusing the youngster. I was asked to role play a store patron who tries to nonviolently disarm the emerging conflict. I should add that these workshops do not give you any "how-to's" beyond helping you to understand some of the nature of conflict and the gestures or approaches that are most likely to fuel or put out the fire. Each role play is unique and the participants are faced with an essentially unknown drama they must deal with creatively on the spot. (Sometimes what one learns from a role play is that you acted in an inappropriate or detrimental way, or sometimes you uncover feelings or responses in yourself you never anticipated.)

I cannot claim any great wisdom as a peacemaker. That's why I was at the workshop. There were role plays that I found myself inadequate to act out. But the grocery store one taught me something wonderful because I *am* very aware of my own parental frustration and embarrassment at having children act out in public. I was the patron. The "mother" and her "child" (roleplayed in fact by my own daughter) were escalating the pitch of their encounter. The "child" was petulant, uncooperative, she was taking things off shelves, she knocked a display down. The "mother" carrying the burdens of the day, began by nagging, then angrily screaming at, then slapping her child around. All I could think of was how well I knew that feeling of being exhausted, embarrassed, experiencing a lack of control. I moved in and commented in a friendly way that I knew just what that was like, I had three of my own. (My instinctive response was nothing more than what had been offered me by understanding fellow-parents at other rocky moments in my life.) This did, however, defuse the situation. The "mother," not being identified as the "bad one," saved face, recovered, and lightened up. She scolded the child once more, then seemed content to let the episode pass by.

The workshop leaders indicated that they had never witnessed the scene played out in quite that way. (I must add they had done that role play only a few times.) Usually, they said, the focus had been on the safety of the child, and on trying to divert the attention of the "perpetrator of violence" in order to protect the innocent. Various ploys had been used. But this time the whole issue was cast differently for I, as the intervenor, had identified with the violent one, not the innocent. And my concern for her feelings and her concerns reached into the dark twisted pain of the conflict and let light flood in.

What I learned from that role play was that the ministry of healing presence does call us not only to recognize the essential goodness and light of each person but to recognize in ourselves the same darkness we wish to dispel in others.

Forgiveness

There is a mystery which, I think, is at that heart of the spiritual vitality of familied life itself. That is the mystery of forgiveness that on more than one occasion has been called the central dynamic of family spirituality. Forgiveness is not simply saying "I'm sorry." (Nor is it, in the spirit of a popular love story of several years ago, "never having to say you're sorry.") Forgiveness is the liberating fruit of the Easter event.

During the Easter season Christians liturgically remember the events that followed Jesus' Crucifixion and Resurrection from the dead. They recall his appearances to his disciples and learn anew from them the truth and the meaning of "the things that happened during these last days." One of my favorites is the account of John (20:19–23) in which Jesus is depicted as entering through the closed doors of the room in which the fearful disciples gather. He speaks words of peace to them, proclaiming that he has come to send them forth in the same way in which he was sent forth by God. He then breathes into them the Holy Spirit (in a gesture reminiscent of the Spirit-filled confirmation of Jesus at the baptism in the Jordan) and says, "For those whose sins you forgive, they are forgiven: for those whose sins you retain, they are retained" (20:23).

The power of the resurrected Christ! To loosen the bondage of sin. The power of human choice! To choose to hold in bondage those to whom you refuse forgiveness. The creative capacity of divinity itself for the transformation of human community lies in our hands in the mystery of forgiveness.

As Easter people, we are called to move from the dark realm of sin—all in us and our relationships that ensnares our true freedom and dignity as children of God—to the spacious, light-filled life. The key is forgiveness. Again, to forgive is not to blind oneself to sin, or "make allowances." No, outrage is essential. But our outrage must contain the knowledge that the very sin from which we so recoil is no stranger to our own hearts. We are all dark as well as light, needing to be redeemed, needing to redeem each other.

To image the dynamics of forgiveness in terms of light and dark is to see ourselves (the forgivers) as knowing our own capacity for darkness yet choosing the light and extending to others the opportunity to do the same. We have this powerful recreative gift as part of our inheritance. We can free ourselves and others from the terrible bondage that warps the image of God within.[2]

It may seem hopelessly naive to claim that when we genuinely forgive one another, we actually change the nature of reality. Yet as Christians we at least pay lip service to the claim that love is indeed stronger than death.

An unlikely story comes to mind as an illustration of this point. It is the story of Maria Goretti, a young Italian girl officially made a saint in 1950. She is not a figure who holds much popular appeal for late twentieth-century American Catholics. But the reason she was made a saint is germane here. Maria Goretti was a pious preteen living in a little Italian peasant village around the turn of this century. She entered puberty early and her budding femininity attracted the attention of a nearby neighbor boy of twenty, Alessandro. He began to lust after Maria. One day, overwhelmed by his passion, he dragged her off her front porch into an upstairs room where he tried to rape her. She resisted fiercely. He threatened her with a knife. She continued to resist. Angered, he attacked her viciously. She lived for less than a day. As she was dying, Maria forgave her attacker.

This depressing tale has entered the official records of sanctity not because Maria Goretti preserved her virginity at all costs (although the era in which her canonization took place did put a great value on purity), but because she forgave the one who so horribly wronged her.

And Maria's story only really begins here. For the offering of forgiveness also means that forgiveness must be accepted, that darkness be admitted and seen for what it is and the light allowed to pierce through. There is in the act of forgiving a quality that invites such a response. Maria's murderer was sentenced to a long prison term at hard labor. For many years he remained unrepentant and hostile. Then Alessandro had a dream in which Maria herself appeared to him, offering him forgiveness once again. So changed was he by this apparition that he became repentant and allowed himself to be reborn to a new and changed life. After his release from prison, he became a gardener at a nearby church where Maria's mother worked as housekeeper. In later years they received communion at the altar rail side by side.

I certainly do not want to be misunderstood as in any way condoning what Alessandro did or even suggesting that the appropriate response to such evil is a simpering "It's all right." It is *not* all right. And the outrage and anger of all who have been victimized are just and, as I have said, an essential part of bringing the darkness of our lives into the light.

But the light is in the end utterly transformative. At some point, when the injustice of what has occurred has been named and recognized in its full horror, it is then time for the healing process to begin. Forgiveness is the key. "Peace be with you. For those whose sins you forgive, they are forgiven: For those whose sins you retain, they are retained." The sins of violence and abuse hold in bondage not only those who inflict them but those on whom they are inflicted. Its darkness blinds all involved. Outrage and confrontation begins to illuminate its contours. The Easter power of forgiveness brings it into the full light of day, transfiguring what was once seemingly opaque in the visible light of divine life itself.

Families are, first and foremost, Easter people. They are communities called to offer and accept forgiveness together. Opportunities occur daily because family members live in such close proximity. The demands of simply being together call forth innumerable occasions for husband, wife, parent, child, brother, sister, and in-laws to admit that they have hurt and failed one another, to ask for forgiveness, to acknowledge that there has been hurt, and to freely offer to forgive. Beyond that, family life sometimes calls us to seek, receive, acknowledge the need for, and offer the gift of forgiveness in the midst of searing pain and the anguish of betrayal. We are called out of darkness into the Tabor light.[3]

> Let us walk in the light of the Lord
> Let us sing of his love through all the earth
> We are still on our way, we are going home together
> Let us walk in the light of the Lord.[4]

·10·

The bathroom and the bedroom, nestled as they are in the intimate recesses of the home, are the rooms most likely to contain mirrors. There are mirrors in other parts of the dwelling as well—over the mantelpiece, on the back of a parlor door—but the mirrors in these common areas are not used in the same way mirrors are in the private realms of the family. The mirrors of the inner home are symbols of the self-examination that may or may not go on in the innermost hearts of family members. Mirrors reflect us back to ourselves. We may choose to look closely or we may prefer to pose before our reflections, concerning ourselves primarily with the facade of self we hope to construct and present to the world.

Traditional Christian formation—the discipline of reshaping the individual into the image of likeness of God—assumed that there are certain "virtues" or character traits that are both catalysts for and acquired in the process of being reformed in the divine image. Beyond the virtues are other states and attitudes of being that are believed to facilitate the process of restoration of the image of God within. The three most famous, institutionalized in the monastic world as religious vows, were poverty, chastity, and obedience. Corresponding to the virtues were attitudes—the "vices"—felt to be inimical to Christian formation. The vices were qualities of character to be purged or avoided by those seeking to lead a God-centered life.

Outside of some specifically monastic or clerical context, our modern Christian sensibilities have little interest in the traditional virtues, vices, or vows. Yet we still concern ourselves with authentic Christian living and so recast the virtues and vices into contemporary parlance.

In older artistic renderings of the "vices," vanity was often represented as a woman admiring herself in a mirror. The negative preoccupation with the external self that this scene depicts was thought, in the eyes of our cultural forebears, to distract one from true reflection on the inner self—the soul. I'm not sure that a contemporary Christian critique would depict the "sin" of exteriority in this way. The grievous neglect of intangible realities for the lure of the external bears the name "materialism" today: squanderous consumption, keeping up with fads, buying more and better houses, cars, stereos, VCR's, hot tubs, designer clothing, imported toys, gourmet food and kitchen utensils, computers, jewelry, etc. The piles of catalogs published in a year in this country, advertising more and better things to consume, would fill the most spacious of cathedrals. One Christian commentator has decried these "idols of the marketplace." We may not speak today of vanity as such, but we deplore the underlying sin as vehemently as did our grandmothers and grandfathers.[1]

And what of families? What are the virtues and vices that Christian families can acquire or shun so that they grow into the divine likeness? It is common, and thought to be psychologically sound, for today's parents to provide their preschool daughters and sons with toy mirrors into which they can peer and see themselves reflected. The recognition, "That's Sarah," or "That's Jacob," or "That's me" is assumed to be an important step in ego development needed for healthy maturation. That today's parents at the same time provide mirrors for themselves or their older children that facilitate a self-reflection based on Christian norms is not so clear.

The problem here is, in part, one of translating the traditional language of formation into the family idiom. It does not seem to me that our inheritance—which so often was articulated from a celibate male context—makes much sense for those whose life experience is very different, without such reinterpretation and translation.

One thing, however, is clear. Self-reflection, both individual and communal, is utterly necessary for any continuing growth into the image and likeness of God. We need mirrors in which to see ourselves and in front of which we honestly attempt to fashion a self that is pleasing not to crowds or neighbors but pleasing in the eyes of God.

A Vowed Life

We intend to establish a school for the Lord's service. In
drawing up its regulations, we hope to set down nothing
harsh, nothing burdensome. The good of all concerned,
however, may prompt us to a little strictness in order to
amend faults and to safeguard love. As we progress in this
way of life and in faith, we shall run on the path of God's
commandments, our hearts overflowing with the
inexpressible delight of love. Never swerving from his
instructions, then, but faithfully observing his teachings in
the monastery until death, we shall through patience share
in the sufferings of Christ that we may deserve also to share
in his kingdom.

Rule of Saint Benedict, prologue

When a woman or man enters a traditional monastic community she or he takes, at least, the three vows of poverty, chastity,
and obedience. These stated promises provide the framework
within which that individual will be schooled in the service of the
Lord Jesus. The vows certainly do not exhaust the fund of varied
experiences that constitute the monastic life; but they are expressive of its values and the way in which our cumulative tradition
has understood how an authentic Christian life is most ably
achieved.

I think of St. Francis of Assisi (who managed to balance quasi-
monastic contemplation with an itinerant mendicancy) joyously
embracing "Lady Poverty" as his bride because she alone could
teach him the kenotic (self-emptying) mystery of the Christ-life
with its naked surrender to the divine. I think, too, of the ecstatic

bridal mysticism of Spain and Germany with its passionate descriptions of the soul's outpourings of love to the divine and of the chastity that marries itself to God alone. I am reminded of the wise admonitions of the Benedictine tradition that teaches an obedient submission to the will of abbot or abbess as training for obedience to the will of God.

What do these vows, so richly explored in the celibate world of monastic life, have to do with life in family? One could say that a monastery creates an intentional family. It has been described as such. Or that what goes on there is analogous to the domestic family. The comparison breaks down when one considers that domestic families are not intentional in the same way as monasteries. You don't choose your natural brothers and sisters. And not all natural family members have a freely chosen "vocation" to Christian living. They are there because they were born there. Similarly, domestic families do not often consist of a grouping of like-minded reasonably mature (and same-sexed) adults. They are more varied than that; they include women, men, the very young, the dependent, those incapable of making mature decisions, the very old, the unwanted, the sick, addicted, and asocial, those you wouldn't invite unless you had to, those without any "vocation" at all.

So for a familied person to draw upon the accumulated spiritual wisdom that is ours as Christians, some cautious translation is required. Certainly poverty, chastity, and obedience are not the only normative categories of religious formation open to the Christian. Faith, hope, and charity are qualities of spiritual character to which all Christians are called. And there is a substantive literature on these from many denominational points of view. But people rarely *vow* faith, hope, and charity as they do poverty, chastity, and obedience. For these last are not simply inner character qualities, they are practices, things you promise to do, the doing of which can (and should) lead to an inner transformation that disposes one to "serve the Lord." Moreover, these three vows are hallowed in the tradition in a special way. They are known as the "evangelical counsels," the unique expressions of holiness that the cumulative wisdom of the Christian tradition for centuries saw as descriptive of the perfect Christ-life. "Be ye perfect, just as I am perfect" echoed in the ears of Christendom. The community saw the most authentic response to this call mirrored in the embrace of poverty, chastity, and obedience. I find it intriguing to explore the question of these three vows within the context of the vows of matrimony and the family that it engenders.

Poverty

As an external practice, Christian poverty is an expression of the religious impulse to rid oneself of all the things that hinder loving, serving and having time for God and neighbor. When we are inordinately in love with our possessions, we become blind to loving God. When our time is consumed in getting more things, we have no time for others. When we are so attached to what we have that we are given over to protecting and maintaining it, we lose both the freedom to serve where there is need and the vision to see beyond our own possessiveness.

Christian teaching on the salutary nature of religious poverty has a distinguished history. Its most notable contemporary exponent is the founder of the American Catholic Worker movement, Dorothy Day. Dorothy Day wrote of this practice:

> Love of brother means voluntary poverty, stripping one's self, putting off the old man, denying one's self, etc. It also means non-participation in those comforts and luxuries which have been manufactured by the exploitation of others. While our brothers suffer from lack of necessities, we will refuse to enjoy comforts. . . . And we must keep this vision in mind, recognize the truth of it, the necessity for it, even though we do not, cannot, live up to it.[1]

It is important to distinguish, as Dorothy Day does, between voluntary and involuntary poverty. The one is a chosen spiritual path, the other an imposed and degrading system that dims the humanity of its victims. Certainly the latter is not advocated by anyone.

But what does voluntary poverty have to do with families? It is one thing for a single person to decide to give away everything she or he owns. It is quite another thing to do if you are responsible for the care of dependents for whom poverty may not represent freedom but an impoverishment of education, medical care, and the protection of an environment that can nurture healthy young life. For alongside the religious impulse to rid oneself of all that stands in the way of God is a parallel (and I think not appreciated but equally religious) impulse to provide, to nest, to shelter, feed, clothe, care for, teach, and provide stability for one's own.

The impulse is a profoundly graced one. One lovely book on the spirituality of family even describes "the sacrament of the care of others" as a primary component of the family's way to God.[2] All pregnant women know that curious nesting and preparing urge that comes just a few weeks before the birth of a child that compels one to clean out drawers, set up the bassinet and make the place ready for caring. Many young parents (and some not so young) know well the inner urgings that turn their attention from the wider world of concerns to the tiny and specific world of their own children. Providing for the youngsters becomes the focus of energy that might otherwise be spent on a wider public. All this is part of the sacramental life of caring. Yet its importance has been overlooked in the traditional rhetoric which has championed radical literal poverty almost to the exclusion of any other option. I think immediately of that great saint, Jerome, who packed his orphaned younger sister off to a convent for life so he could go to the Holy Land and who later praised the widow Paula when she gave away her children's entire inheritance so that she could join him.

Even in contemporary times, the tension between these two impulses in the Catholic Worker movement was felt over and over again with the champions of radical poverty winning out.

Dorothy Day wrote of the communal farms that sprang up under the aegis of the Worker. They did fairly well, she recounts, except for the families that came. For these tended to concern themselves with putting away a nest egg, or taking with them more than they brought to the farms. There was a conflict for families between the communal ethic of pooled resources that drew them to the farms and the felt necessity of providing for their own. Even in Dorothy's own life, this conflict was present. She had a daughter who, because of the sometimes rough environment of the Catholic Worker houses that offered hospitality to the most downtrodden from America's city streets, was educated for a time at a boarding school while her mother ministered in voluntary poverty to the poor.

The radical way voluntary poverty has been lived out in much of the Church's past has prompted this tension. The tradition has drawn the lines too sharply between those who are willing to give up all for the pearl of great price and those who become relegated to the unredeemed masses pursuing wealth and ignoring gospel imperatives. In fact, precisely because the ideal of poverty has been so unremittingly described in bold terms, familied people *do* tend to disregard its call and to give themselves over to an unreflective accumulation of possessions in the name of "providing" that may be in actuality more in harmony with the secular consumer culture than any vision of gospel life.

A few families seem genuinely to be called to an ascetic material witness. What I think the majority of families are called to is not necessarily voluntary poverty but a radical simplicity. Families must distinguish carefully between what they "need" and what they simply "want." A genuine need may be for medical and dental care far beyond the resources of an absolute poverty to provide. But families would do well to evaluate whether the many purchases they make are consistent with genuine needs or simply reflect what they or the neighborhood ethos prompted by media urgings want. Such conscious self-reflection gives a family the opportunity to see itself in a new light.

Parents must honor the very real needs of their own children; at the same time, they must be careful not to ignore the witness of voluntary poverty but rather let its spirit animate the economic choices they make. Those choices become very specific, but there is no one plan of action that is applicable to all families. One family will grapple over whether it is in keeping with simplicity to maintain a house in the country and an apartment in the city. Another family will wrestle with the question: Should they own property at all? And the choices are daily as well as long-term. Parents may struggle to decide whether a coveted but exorbitant toy should be purchased for a birthday as well as about tithing or investing in socially conscious corporations.

There is a vigorous, simple lifestyle movement within all the Christian churches. "Downward mobility" is a catchword for this movement.[3] Each family must decide where the cutting edge is for itself: What simplifies our life, makes us freer to love each other, our Lord, and our neighbor? Which things that we own are idols or more burden than we need to carry? What do we genuinely need to sustain ourselves economically so that we are neither consumed by our consumption nor so impoverished that we do not have the reserves to freely give to one another, to others, and to our God?

Chastity

Chastity has to do with relationships, with how one goes about being with others. It refers to more than abstinence from sexual intercourse. In the sometimes baroque language of our contemplative tradition, religious chastity was often described as a marriage to God. The chaste soul was the soul betrothed not to any human lover but the supreme lover, God, or Christ. To be a bride of such a bridegroom meant that one gave the whole of her or his heart to the divine spouse, "marrying" God, body, heart, and mind. The iconography of medieval Christianity gives ample witness to this phenomenon of spiritual marriage as it depicts the mystical nuptial rites of saints such as Catherine of Siena. Likewise, in many monastic communities the rites of profession to the religious vows were celebrated as "marriages," replete with the wearing of bridal finery and the presentation of a ring.

When a man and woman enter into the marriage convenant they betroth themselves first and foremost to one another. Chastity they do not vow (generally). But, like the monk or nun, they do need to make an intentional commitment regarding their sexuality, their very capacity for relationship, and the fact that they are graced with being either male or female. I would identify the two "vows" that might appropriately be made by familied persons as integrity and fidelity.

The figure of the Virgin Mary hovers like a guardian angel over this first vow of integrity—at least in my own mind. She, in her guise as the Immaculate Conception has come to represent for me what the vow of integrity is all about. In the Mission Church in Santa Barbara where I was a parishioner for many years, there was a painting of Our Lady of Guadalupe, the Patron of the Americas, that hung on the east wall of the church. I used to sit just adjacent to it and, if my mind wandered during the service, I would gaze at this Virgin in the robes of an Aztec princess, the black girdle of pregnancy wrapped around her, her feet resting on the crescent moon. One December 8, the feast of the Immaculate Conception, I was thus strategically placed under Guadalupe's haunting eyes. The homily, given by an elderly friar, was dull and pedagogically inept (at least for my tastes). Mary, he droned on, was by a special dispensation from God conceived in the womb of her Mother Anne free from the taint of mortal sin. She was sinless throughout her life, unlike the rest of us, making her pure flesh the fitting matter from which the spotless flesh of Our Lord was to come.

I turned my attention to Mary. What did it mean for her to be immaculately conceived? What was the mystery of her heart that compelled me, despite the fact that I felt repelled by the good friar's vapid, otherworldly depiction of her. I knew a different

Mary, an earthy young Jewish woman who was so full of wonder and imagination, that she actually *believed* the promises of God, believed them so passionately that they became real in her own flesh. What did it mean for her to be immaculate? The numinous aura that radiated from the figure of Guadalupe was like a mandala, drawing me gradually into the center of the image where Mary's hands were clasped between her breasts. And then I knew. What awesome integrity this young woman had! She belonged so fully and completely to the voice of God within that she was able to hear and to respond completely to its call, no matter how perplexing and challenging it might be. (She was, after all, unmarried when God's messenger came to tell her she was with child, and to be found pregnant and unmarried under Jewish law meant she could be sentenced to death by stoning.)

Mary lived so deeply out of the center of herself (where the human touches the divine) that her integrity was complete, inviolable. Most of us live torn by the many voices that cry out for us to follow—the tempting voices of collective pressure, the voices of friends, family, our own conflicting voices issuing from the unconscious, our egos, our various "selves." We have a hard time being still enough to sort out all the voices. We don't even know how to recognize the whisper that is God's. And here was a simple young carpenter's wife so attuned to the living word that she became the vessel through which that Word was spoken in flesh for the world.

The integrity that family members are called to is modeled by the Virgin of the Immaculate Conception. We are called to live in and amongst others, deeply enmeshed in the reciprocal caring that is family life. But we are called to have a radical integrity that is centered on the voice of God spoken deep in our hearts. While responsive to all the voices that demand our loving attention and time, we must not be deafened by the cacophony of the "family ego," or confused by the din of cultural noise. At the same time we are called to distinguish the authentic voice of God within ourselves from the strident calls of our own conflicting selves. A task of no small proportion! Our model—not a successful corporation executive or a hero of mythic adventures but an obscure young woman who married a poor carpenter, raised a family, and with utter integrity lived out of her deepest self where spoke the Word of God.

Fidelity is the second of the relational virtues called for in family life. This has the obvious meaning of being faithful to wife or husband, reserving the most intimate expressions of love for that one person alone and faithfully maintaining that love you share. Fidelity means more than this, too. It means being faithful to the "us" in a marriage as well as the "you" and "me." It means constantly juggling priorities, being attentive to the use of time and to the good of individuals as well as the whole family. It means being committed to a lifetime that never seems to settle down to an easeful pace, to a community that never leaves you alone, which asks of you more than you can give and gives back more than you could possibly ever receive.

Fidelity cuts deeper than even this, too. To be faithful is to have the integrity that Mary had and to be willing to act on it and take the consequences. Fidelity as a vowed practice in family life is the promise to be there for one another, year after year, with one ear open to the voice of spouse, child, parent, or in-law and the other open to listen to God both "between" the words of this human speech and in the depth of your own heart.

The family is the context within which we who are called to the marital and familied vocation hear the word of God. Much of that voice will come to us through our closest relationships and in our prayers that center around our experiences as family people. The art is to learn fidelity in listening, attentiveness to the levels of discourse that take place in our homes, and in cultivating an ear like Elijah's who mistook wind, earthquake, and fire for the divine voice until he knew he had heard it in a still small voice (1 Kings 19:11, 12).

Obedience

In monastic practice, the rules of the community, like those set forward in the *Rule of St. Benedict,* govern all aspects of an individual's life. The dweller in the monastery is invited to surrender self-will in order to be re-formed by the psychological and spiritual dynamics at work in the form of the rules. This requires that one adopt an obedient attitude that seeks formation. Monastic life is disciplined; this is seen to be good, for inner freedom is not possible without some ordering of the various drives that compel us both interiorly and exteriorly.

Obedience is the willingness to submit one's self-will to the will of God expressed in the wisdom of the monastic rule and of the community superior. Does this translate at all into a practice that can enliven the domestic church? I would say no if obedience is understood in terms of a particular hierarchical structure of family authority, the father/husband generally being on top and everyone else "obeying" his every will and command. My sense is that it would require the wisdom of Solomon for anyone to exercise this kind of authority in a way that would be empowering and freeing for other family members.[4]

But obedience is not an empty idea either and is one that our culture, which glories in instant gratification, the quick fix, and the pursuit of wealth and pleasure, would do well to contemplate again. Obedience implies discipline—but obedience to what and discipline of what?

Our churches and their teachings, especially in their most articulate social forms, give us some clue in this matter. What we, as individuals and families, are invited to be obedient to, is a vision of person and of the world. The vision, which has biblical roots and which has been enunciated recently in the public statements issued by a number of Christian denominations, is a profoundly communal one.[5] It is a vision of ourselves as part of a whole, members of a wider human family brought to birth by God and created to share and steward the resources of one world.

Perhaps the most publicized of these church statements have been those drawn up by the American Catholic bishops, notably their pastoral letters on peace and war, *The Challenge of Peace* and on economics, *Economic Justice for All*. These two documents speak of many specific matters—of the arms race, of hunger, of the just war theory, of the proper use of wealth, etc. Underlying them both is a challenge that is perhaps even more startling to the average Christian than any of the specific proposals that the letters set forth. These documents proclaim a moral vision of personhood and community that is biblically Christian. That vision, if clearly apprehended, is at some variance with the way most of us think about these things.

The economic pastoral begins with an assumption of human dignity which asserts that the person is sacred and the clearest reflection of God among us. Human dignity comes from God, not from nationality, race, sex, economic status, or human accomplishment. The person is not only sacred but social. Human dignity can only be realized and protected in community. God's design gives the human vocation a communitarian nature. Further, all people have a right to participate in the life of society. To be fully human is to exercise one's God-given talents in the service of the whole. Moreover, basic justice demands that people be assured a minimum level of participation. Such participation is not possible unless all are guaranteed basic human rights—not only civil and political (i.e., freedom of speech, worship, the vote, etc.) but also economic rights (life, food, clothing, shelter, rest, medical care, education, and employment). As followers of Christ we are challenged to make this a reality. We are asked to work on behalf of those whose full God-given dignity has been truncated by social and economic marginalization. We must make a fundamental option for the poor. The justice of a society is tested by the treatment of the poor, those who have been pushed to the margins of social viability.

The peace pastoral also begins with an assumption of the dignity and worth of all human life. Violence in all its forms·disfigures the image of God in humankind. As disciples of Christ, the bringer of peace, we are required to seek for ways to make the forgiveness, justice, love, and mercy of God visible in a world where violence is the norm. War, especially, is decried. Yet there also exists the responsibility to protect the peace. Under certain limited conditions (according to the traditional just war theory), war is lamentably permissible to protect innocent life and basic human rights. Yet new moral issues are raised with the development of nuclear technology. Now that modern weapons pose the possibility of widespread and indiscriminate destruction, moral justification of nuclear conflict must be strongly questioned. Questions are also raised about the morality of deterrence as a long-term basis for the peace toward which we as Christians must work.

These two letters raise important questions that must be taken seriously. They particularly challenge families to reflect on their roles as builders of a just and peaceful world—both within the family and through the family's extended community. Especially as the primary teachers of and formative influence on their children, how do families live out and pass on this Christian perspective? A wide panoply of issues emerges to confront the Christian family: the just and peaceful structure of family life, the conscientious gain and use of money with an eye to an option for the poor, the use of methods other than violence to solve problems, teaching family members about discrimination based on race or sex, religion, age, or physical or economic handicap, teaching as well about abortion and the death penalty. The list goes on and on.

In the monastic school of the Lord's service, obedience to the rules of community is essential. What kind of obedience must families practice? I would answer this very broadly: obedience to the wide and radical vision of the biblical imperative that affirms the dignity of the human person can only be realized in community, a vision that sees humankind as a whole, not as separate competing individuals, nations, ideologies, or interest groups. We must live this and teach this. If we begin this awesome task, we will find our most closely held assumptions and opinions challenged. We will be forced to really scrutinize our own visions of the human person and the world community. Are the underlying assumptions we make about who we are formed by our faith, or are they rooted in a cultural perception that is antithetical to gospel values? How much are we "of the world" or "not of the world," to phrase the question in the traditional way?

The struggle to discern the root source of our orientation to reality has always been part of our Christian history. In the third and fourth centuries zealous Christians in large numbers fled the cities and centers of civilization for the deserts of Egypt and Palestine. They located themselves on the margins of society, able to look from that distance with new eyes on the values that the civilized world held dear. These hermits sought to be remade, purged of the sins of greed, luxury, and self-aggrandizement that motivated human activity in "the world." They moved to the desert where, symbolically, human community could once again be re-created out of the chaos of wilderness into the image of the new Adam born in Christ. "Worldly" values identified with the structures of civilization and "worldly" values in the form of demons discovered in the self were fought and overcome in the desert. There a new world began with each hermit father or mother ushering in the divine creativity through the reformation of self.

The struggle is still with us. Although we no longer (and should not) disdain "the world" in the sense that we perceive spirit and matter to exist in two opposing camps, we still must be born again in the womb of the gospel. What our Scriptures and tradition offer us is not a comfortable vision of self and community that simply upholds our cultural mores. Far from it. There is still a real tension between the world and the Christian message. We are challenged to examine all areas of our lives, both public and private, moving a bit to the margins for a fresh view, raising questions, fighting demons, recreating the world anew.

LOOKING
OUT

·11·

Even the most intimate recesses of the home have windows on the periphery that look out on a world larger than the one contained within the home's four walls. And in the common areas windows are often a prominent architectural feature. In a modern home they may reach from floor to ceiling, affording an expansive view of neighborhood or verdant valley. In an urban apartment complex, windows may give one a view only of the shaded windows of the adjacent building.

While the owners of homes with many windows may bemoan the fact when spring-cleaning comes round once more, they know that a home (or any building for that matter) without windows is an aberrant sight. There is something even sinister about a windowless structure, something that broods and suggests evil. Prison cells, designed for psychological privation, restrict the flow of sunlight and air through tiny slits or do away with windows altogether. In contrast, a home with many openings to the outside (although sometimes shaded or draped for privacy) is a welcoming sight. Sunlight streams into the rooms, fresh air circulates. There is something healthful and life-giving about the window that suggests the profound and necessary relationship between the inner and outer, the private shelter and the commonly shared out-of-doors, between the domestic and the public realms.

A family does not exist in isolation. Its full experience is derived not only from its intimate life but from its relation to others as well. The family as a complex, multigenerational and many-membered entity exists in a network of other families. The family's Christian commitment must be expressed inside and outside the family circle. The home looks out on the world. The windows are its eyes.

155

Circles of Care

As the lives of individuals as different as Martin Luther
King and Mother Teresa of Calcutta remind us, when the
mutual love of families and friends is authentic it does not
remain absorbed in an *egoisme à deux* or three or more,
but reaches out beyond itself to the neighbor, not to
"humanity," but to the concrete person in need, whoever or
wherever that person is.

Walter Conn, *Christian Conversion*

The night before he died, with all the sorrow and sense of impending dread that must have haunted him, Jesus met with his friends in an upper room in a house in Jerusalem to share a meal. There he knelt and washed their feet, the way a servant might. As he did so he told his companions that he wanted them to follow his example. He wanted them to love one another the way he had loved them.

Every person in a family who has bathed feet, bandaged wounds, carried the young, tended the elderly, wiped dripping noses and chafed bottoms knows something of the tender care of which Jesus spoke that night nearly two thousand years ago. To serve one another and to love one another—those are the injunctions given to all Christians that define the apostolate of the domestic church. Most family members, even without the Christian imperatives, certainly experience this as a central part of their vocation. That the service and love that characterize life within the domestic circle must also spill out into the wider circle of the world community is not so obvious to many. This overflow of love must amount to more than "charity," a sort of good-hearted distribution of what is leftover when we have spent the bulk of our reserves caring for ourselves and those closest to us.

For a long time this concept has haunted me. It took root many years ago in the form of a dream—my "Franciscan dream"—that has served as an iconic touchstone through which I have understood much of the process of my own spiritual life. In the dream, I was in the choir loft of the Mission Church in Santa Barbara (which was, in fact, our parish church at the time). A guitarist friend and I were responsible for beginning the liturgy with an opening song. We started but couldn't get the attention of the congregation below. There was a disturbance. We looked down and saw a number of unruly children banging the kneelers and rattling rosaries. To quiet this outburst and get things started, we decided to go downstairs into the aisle and process in, singing loudly. That didn't work either. The liturgy couldn't begin.

Then I was no longer the song leader coming into the church from the back; I was standing behind the pulpit. My perspective was changed. In front of me were pews full of complacent looking men and women dressed in sumptuous finery: furs, expensive jewelry, chic dresses, and handsome suits. I was to preach to them and was full of passion to do so. I think I was wearing a simple sacklike garment, perhaps even the robes of a friar. I was exhorting them to give. No, I said, don't just take out your checkbooks and give what is leftover. You need to give, not out of your excess, but out of your necessity! Then I began to show them what this meant. I began to take off the clothes I was wearing. This was an invitation for them to do the same. The removal of my shoes was significant; I needed to strip them off and stand barefoot on the ground.

This dream has taught me well over the years. I have learned a lot about myself through it. But two features that have stood out and been recurrently important are my admonition that "you need to give, not out of excess but out of necessity" and the gesture of removing my shoes. What *does* it mean to give out of necessity? Is it that to which we are called? What has this to do with standing on bare ground?

The last of these questions was answered for me some time after the occurrence of the dream when I recalled the story of Moses on Mt. Horeb that occurs in the third chapter of Exodus. The Bible recounts how Moses had come to the mountain with the flock he was tending. He was startled by an angel who appeared to him in a flaming bush that was not consumed by its fire. Curious, Moses approached the site but was warned, "Do not come near; put off your shoes from your feet, for the place on which you are standing is holy ground" (Ex. 3:5). Yes, holy ground. Not only was the sanctuary in which I stood to preach holy ground, but also the very earth upon which my congregation, separated from its sacred touch by the soles of their expensive shoes, walked.

To strip down to the point where we can genuinely touch the holiness of creation means we need to peel off the layers of ourselves that keep us covered. To give out of excess, to simply open our purses and write out a check, is not at all to give in the radical way to which we are called. No, we need to give of heart and mind, of flesh and bone, out of the very marrow of our existence.

The Domestic Circle

What does this mean for familied people? My dream, of course, was mine and spoke specifically to the state of my psyche and its needs. But the message seems to me to go beyond myself. For it is in family that I, at least, have come closest to the kind of giving out of necessity of which I think this Franciscan dream spoke. If only because of the constant drain on physical and emotional reserves, family life teaches one how to give when there is nothing left. When what you have is not even enough for self-maintenance, then your giving is carved out of what is necessary. Patience, wisdom, attention, flexibility, humor, good judgment, firm but loving direction: how often these run dry and we as familied people are called upon to find some drop left at the bottom of our reserves or, if that is not possible, to acknowledge our shortcomings and ask to be given these in return.

We learn to give out of necessity within the domestic circle. This is a precious instruction, for it gentles us and makes our giving gracious. There is a vast reservoir of this capacity to give among those who have raised or are raising families. I have experienced this on the retreats I have directed, especially for women. I see it in the parishes and congregations that I am privileged to visit. What strikes me is that many women, especially once the intense period of mothering in early childhood is past, have developed skills and a love of doing for others that continues to overflow. It often gets expressed in volunteer work. How many dozens of church bazaars offer crocheted knickknacks and baked goods which represent the loving labor of hundreds of hours? How many times have I listened to earnest conversations about redecorating a bathroom or finding just the right color-coordinated towels for the kitchen that reflect the nesting and providing instinct natural to family life? How often I have seen grandmothers lavishly spend time and money delighting their grandchildren?

These manifestations of intimate and caring concern for particular people, generally within the small circle of family or church, are lovely. I sometimes wonder why this type of human sensibility generally seems to be limited to the "private" spheres of home or immediate community? Why don't our civic and political lives reflect this same kind of nurturing concern for the individual? Why does our "charity" often restrict itself to a dainty dipping into our purses or holding a rummage sale for some "safe" (albeit genuinely important) charitable cause?

With apologies to the many Christians who do roll up their sleeves and dig elbow and chin deep into the work of caring for the world, I would insist that many families need to look beyond the circle of their own personal cares to respond to their brothers, sisters, children and parents in the wider circle of God's human family with the skills of loving attentiveness they have learned.

Widening the Circle

Parents are the first teachers of their children. We may send our kids off to school for the 3R's and to music and dance academies for aesthetic instruction, but they learn most about who they are and how the world is put together from us. They learn this almost by osmosis. They learn it by assimilating our attitudes toward ourselves and the domestic and global families of which we are a part. Sometimes the immediate life of the family seems only remotely concerned with the big issues of the world, and the big issues are left for "big people" (especially those in positions of leadership) to be concerned about. Certainly in our complex world, children cannot be expected to grasp the totality of our political, economic, and social realities. How many adults can? But these big issues do have small manifestations that touch us daily in family life. Parents can explore these as teaching moments or avail themselves of the many small ways natural in family life to let the attitude of domestic caring spill out into a larger sphere.

There are three simple things, at least, that parents can teach their children: the beauty and variety of the human family; the suffering of that family; and that we as families can act in many ways to alleviate suffering and restore the dignity of all God's people. Such lessons would do much to create a generation of Christians whose compassion is aroused by the miracle of God's creation, our world, and its inhabitants.

Learning Beauty and Variety

There seems to be an inbred tendency in people to fear and dislike things with which they are not familiar. Small children will often recoil at the sight of a severely disabled person simply because they have never seen someone like her before. Older children are likely to taunt and exclude a new classmate whose unfamiliar language or dress makes him stand out from the crowd. Yet discrimination of any kind is one of the root evils of our world that keeps us from living in true community. A person's relationship with God and with all other people is so linked together that Scripture says, "Whoever does not love, does not know God" (1 John 4:8).

There are innumerable ways families can help break down barriers of discrimination for themselves and their children. The key is familiarity. The areas of possible discrimination are many: race, ethnic or national origin, religion, age, sex, economic status, physical endowments, etc. I remember learning about the ancient and mysterious beauty of the Native American way of life from my mother who was involved in the Indian Center in Los Angeles many years ago. She would bring home brightly painted and feathered kachina dolls and tell me stories about the kachina rituals in which she had participated on the mesas in the Southwest desert. My mother taught me about the delicate art of sandpainting—how the making of each painting was really a prayer and how its practitioners undertook the painting with humility and a sense of being channels for a cosmic ritual that was being enacted.

The appreciation of others whose cultures are different from our own is not tangential to our Christian faith. If we take seriously the claim that humankind was created in the image of God, we will see the many human expressions of God's face, the many fruits of the incarnate labors of God's hands, in the variety that surrounds us. We do not, as families, have to go on a world tour to see the diversity of God's human ways.

One of the best things that happened to me and my own children in California was to participate in some of the rituals celebrated by Jewish neighbors. My children watched their playmates reverently light the candles of the Menorah and recall the history of the Jewish people. They felt something of the deep faith that moved this family and always will carry that memory with them as an insight into a faith tradition that is not their own. I hope the experience will serve as a basis from which my children can evaluate discriminatory comments or attitudes.

Contact is the key to breaking down any discrimination. Regular visits to a rest home for the elderly, volunteer participation in the Special Olympics that celebrate the athletic achievements of persons with disabilities, genuine participation (not just tourism) in the cultural and creative life of people whose ethnic and religious practices are different from our own—all of these (and many others) are a family's teaching means to expanding the circle of care.[1]

Learning of Suffering

As the circle widens, families find that not only is the human family wonderfully various but that it suffers deeply. While none of us want to see our own children suffer, to shield them from or fail to expose them to the suffering of their brothers and sisters is to fail to offer them the depth of the Christian faith. As followers of Christ, we are challenged (in the words of the bishops of the Latin American Catholic Church) to make an "option for the poor," to speak for the voiceless, to defend the defenseless, to feed the hungry, to clothe the naked, shelter the homeless, visit the prisoner.

There are so many ways a family can respond to these challenges that can easily fit into its routine life. A monthly commitment to serve in a soup kitchen, a family letter written on behalf of someone unjustly imprisoned for race or religion, regularly helping an elderly shut-in with grocery shopping, "sponsoring" a child from overseas through one of several organizations (and keeping in touch), helping to find housing for a homeless family, and on and on. All of these activities must be undertaken not with a sense of "doing something for those less fortunate" but with a sense of extending our care to our extended family. The point is, for children (and many adults, myself included), it is important to have real faces and real lives at the other end of our compassion. A check or a bag of canned goods sent off to the anonymous poor may briefly alleviate a little suffering but does not touch us deeply. We need to be converted from our accustomed self-complacency to the real and earnest fact that any human suffering is *our* suffering. As an ecologically, economically, and spiritually interdependent world family, we cannot but be alive to this truth. Our efforts to alleviate this suffering must spring from this realization. When we see giving as something we do out of "excess," we betray our belief that there is an "us" and a "them" and that charity requires us to give them a bit of ours now and then. When we see giving as something that comes from our "necessity," we testify to our grasp of the interconnected world, God's world, of which our family is one essential but not isolated part. How we expose our children to the world's suffering can make the difference in how they (and we) learn to widen the circle of care.

The difference is dramatic. I had, as a child, often given Thanksgiving offerings in church or school that well-intentioned adults would collect and distribute to some unknown "poor" somewhere "out there." But one year I went with my mother to deliver the fixings for a holiday meal to the Native American families that came to the Indian Center. I usually had seen these people at the center done up in ceremonial dress for a special occasion. My mother was not only appreciative of the richness of Indian culture, she was sensitive to the suffering of contemporary Indians and alert to some of the root causes for this problem. She told me how many tribes had been forced to live on reservations of scanty and unyielding land that offers little meaningful or productive work. Many of the men migrated to the cities looking for some employment, but uneducated and unskilled (because training was not available on the reservations), they were forced to take menial jobs. Landlords exploited them, charging enormous rents for substandard housing. If their families were with them in the cities, they lived in squalor, without proper diet or access to adequate medical care. Demoralization like an ugly cloud hung over the Native American family.

We went into the tenements of central Los Angeles looking for the designated apartment, bearing our grocery bags full of cheerfully labeled canned goods and all the festive extras for a middle-class American Thanksgiving feast. The backstairs we were forced to climb were dingy and filthy. I remember especially the unbearable stench of urine that permeated the stairwell (the plumbing in the building was antique and frequently out of order). After a laborious climb we found ourselves at the right doorway.

A silent, tired woman of undefined age let us in. Her apartment was nearly bare of furniture, a dilapidated four-poster sitting in the main room seemed to be the sleeping place of a half-dozen, half-clad children who stood looking at us with worried eyes. We put our bags on the scarred top of a table with three-and-a-half legs. I saw nothing that looked like a stove in the alcove that was the kitchen. It was unbearably sad. I remember wondering, even at my young age, what will these people eat after they consume what is in our bags? There seemed to be no food on the bare and doorless kitchen shelves. Overwhelmed by the smell of poverty, feeling unforgivably fortunate, embarrassed by the contents of our containers with their overflow of non-nutritive "treat" foods (like miniature marshmallows and candied fruits) in which the privileged and well-nourished indulge, I wanted nothing more than to flee from that place.

Yet I have never forgotten it. And I have never forgotten that those native people with their deep wisdom of the earth, their highly developed aesthetics, and beautiful culture were, through the vagaries of historical circumstances, now subsisting in unspeakable conditions in the labyrinth of the city that was my own backyard.

Learning That Families Can Do Something

The world in which we find ourselves is both a beautiful and a terrifying place. We have the responsibility not only to learn to see and give thanks for all that is good; we must also mourn the wounded and dying face of God that is all around us. Our mourning is necessary and should not paralyze us if we allow our grief and anger to flow out in acts of love and acts of resistance.

For families to teach children that there is suffering is simply not enough. We must also be filled with hope that our small efforts can indeed help change the way things are. We can resist evil in all the forms in which it comes, blatant or disguised.

One of the major ways families do this is by taking a counter-cultural stance against the values of a society that rewards greed, avarice, and shows a callous disregard for the dignity of human life. We have spoken of the importance of simplicity of lifestyle. While each family must decide for itself just what this means, it would seem essential to consciously resist the campaigns of clothing companies so that precious time and money are not squandered accumulating designer wardrobes that will be outmoded in a season and to refuse the advertising enticements of the creators of gewgaws and gimmicks that fill the house. These are hard tensions for families who live in neighborhoods where all the other kids at school indulge in apparel that has planned obsolescence sewn in alongside the name labels and status among adults is measured by a materialistic yardstick.

To teach children not only the meaning of money but the spiritual price of acquisitiveness is an uphill battle in our consumer society. My ten-year-old recently complained to us that we *never* did really great things like the other girls' parents, like spending the day at the opulent shopping mall (which she declared was her favorite place in the world!) That the mall is colorful and jazzy, I had to admit. To move against the current of contemporary American life that considers consumption necessary for self-esteem and entertainment is hard. Even the "most fun" things that my children tell me there are to do cost tremendous amounts of money. A visit to a "family fun center" with endless rows of enticing games, each of which requires at least a quarter, can blow an average working person's paycheck in an afternoon.

As equally pervasive as the spirit of materialism and acquisitiveness in our culture is the callous spirit of disregard for the dignity of the person that we see imaged daily in the media. We are "entertained" by the sight of charismatic heroes suavely mutilating and obliterating opponents with arsenals of technologically sophisticated weaponry. We are sold cars, beer, and chewing gum by images of beauty, success, and power that are promised us in advertisements that promote these products.

We are surrounded by images that are in opposition to the image of human dignity given to us by our faith. That faith tells us that we are beloved children of God, each unique in the dignity of our personhood, each called to recognize this belovedness in him/herself and in others and to form a community of care that celebrates and acts to realize the fullness of this reality. The media that so dominates the visual field of the American family projects images of a very different kind.

We sometimes think of TV, films, magazines, and books as just entertainment; commercial advertising is just a means of selling a product. We, as a society, too often consider images to be basically neutral, something that can "catch the eye." For us seeing is a passive act, something peripheral to who we are. Other historical periods have not been quite so sanguine about images. We all know old-fashioned stories about pregnant women being warned not to *look* at harmful or frightful things for fear the child they were carrying might be deformed by the impact of the sight. Not many of us know that for much of Western history it was thought that the eye's energy in the dynamic act of seeing went out and took the shape of the object being viewed. Because of this the soul was thought to be affected in fundamental and structural ways by having the objects of vision imprinted on it. Images were known to be *formative*. Such insights are worth reconsidering.[2]

Preschool children in this country are estimated to spend as much as sixty percent of their waking lives watching television. What images of the person, or relationships between persons, are being presented on much of TV? Do superheroes, Gobots, and Rambo offer meaningful models for human dignity? Do they reflect a respect for life and portray a community of mutual compassion and care?

Does the advertising that enters our homes and surrounds us in our daily lives depict us as uniquely gifted in our individuality? Or are we failures if we do not wear Sassoon jeans, ooze erotic energy through a new perfume, or have the latest toy or model car or computer software? Do our educational institutions, our corporations, our professions project images of people who are important solely because they hold degrees, amass titles, assume power, wield influence, and control wealth? Are we defined by what we "have" materially, educationally, professionally? What about who we are and what we are meant to be?

As parents we offer resistance to these deeply formative images. We can monitor TV watching. We can be sure that we discuss with our children our concerns about what they see. We can provide literature and media that present alternative images of the human person for our children to watch. Our own family has chosen not to have a TV at all. When people ask us, in amazed tones, how we can live without one, we are equally amazed because it seems so normal not to have one that we can't imagine life with TV anymore.

We can offer other sorts of resistance to values that are culturally normative and that contribute so much to the suffering and dehumanization of the human family. We have done our own little part in this regard by trying to participate in economic boycotts. Our children become aware of our efforts because our buying habits are altered during the times we are avoiding a certain product or products of companies whose employees are striking or effecting a boycott because of unfair or dangerous working conditions. For years we have not purchased grapes not only because the migrant workers who do most of the harvesting work under deplorable conditions have not been allowed to form unions but also because growers continue to use toxic pesticides on plants that have produced an alarming rise in the rate of infant mortality and birth defects among the offspring of pregnant women who labor in the fields (for a scanty wage).

For a long time I was never sure if this stance would just seem perverse to our children. Then one day my husband showed up with a letter which my eldest daughter had given him to address and send. It was written during a time we were observing a boycott on Campbell's soups because of a strike levied by the workers in the tomato fields. The letter read:

Feb. 11, 86
1:10 pm

Dear President of Campbells Soup,
   I like your soup, but my Daddy refuses to buy me it because you do not pay your workers enough. Please pay your workers enough so I can eat it.

Sincerely,
Emily Frances

P.S.   In the long run you'll be paying yourself.

At the bottom she had drawn three children's faces with smiles and tongues smacking, a steaming bowl of soup, and an opened Campbell's can.

Children whose parents actively work toward changing and challenging the world not only grow up with a sense that they themselves can act to bring about change; they are also less fearful and feel less powerless when confronted with the staggering facts of today's world (which they cannot long avoid).

I am not naive enough to suggest that if we simply teach our children to write letters of complaint that the vast and entrenched evils of the world will come tumbling down. What I do suggest is that the teaching of a Christian parent must include teaching that human resources and the outrage of the heart are forces to be reckoned with in the ongoing resistance against all that would swallow the God-given image of dignity with which we are each and together endowed. We must let our children know not only that they matter but that the stirrings of conscience with which they are gifted are given to them so that they can be cocreators with God.

If we teach them the awesome mystery of the person, created in the divine image, we can begin to awaken their own sense of responsibility for the preservation of that image in others and to awaken their own potential for Christ-centered action. That lesson (coupled with our own sense of our ultimate dependence on God and our grasp of the fact that we are not demigods hell-bent on having things just the way we think they ought to be right now, but simply cocreators with a loving Creator), can give our children hope for a future in which they are neither ciphers in an impersonal system nor demigods enamored of their own power. And hope is what we must give them, hope in the ultimate goodness of this world into which they have been born, hope in the underlying presence which sustains it, hope in the purpose for which they have been created.

·12·

The domestic family and the world family are open to one another through the windows of the home. Similarly, indoors and outdoors, the intimate environment and the ecosystem that surrounds all life are brought together, symbolically and actually, in the garden. Whether it takes the form of a spacious lawn on a suburban estate or of the cheery marigolds that sprout from the window boxes of a city apartment, the garden is an essential part of the home.

Gardens are spaces of inhabiting. In them the cyclic and ever-maturing mysteries of planting, tending, and harvesting take place. In them we become tender to our earth. In them we know the interdependent nature of God's creation: soil, rain, compost, sun, the labors of our hands all cooperate together. In the garden we are not merely stewards of creation, we are midwives or nursemaids entrusted with the very continuity of life itself. Our job is not to oversee, or control, but to plant, prune, water, feed, and encourage growth. We either make of the garden a verdant refreshing oasis or a desert, stripped of nutrients and barren of new life.

The convergence of the garden with the art of caretaking so central to family spirituality was made clear to me several years ago by a student in one of my classes. During a discussion about the "sacred spaces" of family, a young woman from a large, very traditional, Catholic family spoke up. The garden, she said, had become her family's most sacred space, especially in the years since her mother's death. The mother, a devout and earnest parent, had been the spiritual hub of their large clan. This mother had a wonderful garden that she tended with the same attentiveness she gave to her children. After her death, when most of the children were in their teens, this family discovered that whenever two or three family members would meet to discuss anything of importance or to share heartfelt talk, they would gravitate to the garden. There they would walk and talk. Only gradually did they begin to see this emerging practice as the way in which they gathered in the presence of their mother, who in her planting, pruning, and watering, had given them physical and spiritual life. She was in the garden and as they walked there together, they knew themselves to be in the presence of a source of nurturance greater than their own.

This one family's garden in which the living walked together in a mutual exchange of love, inhabited by the spirit of the caring mother, speaks to me of one of the deepest and most sacred dimensions of the life of the covenanted people. As God's people we, the Church, are bearers of Christ's very life into the world. We are called to be many things. We are gifted by the Spirit in many ways so that the fullness of God's love might be made real and vibrant among us. Of all the calls that are issued to us, it is the call to be peacemakers that seems the most urgent for the Church today.

In my mind that call is not issued on the battlefield or at the starting point of a hero's impossible journey. It is heard instead in the garden. It is known in the patient labors of cultivation. It is seen when dry desert land becomes fertile soil. It is felt when trees hang heavy with fruit, when human toil has been put to the gentle care of new life. It is sensed when a walk among spring violets is treasured as a high and human undertaking. Peacemaking is a call that has been discerned when our gardens' ripeness shows that we have learned that we inhabit one great garden, our earth, when we have learned that we are but one interwoven fabric of created life charged with mutual and tender cultivation by the one who gave and gives us life.

A Place of Springs

Happy those who live in your house
    and can praise you all day long;
And happy the pilgrims inspired by you
    with strength to climb the heights!
As they go through the desolate valley,
    they make it a place of springs,
Clothed in blessings by early rains.

Psalm 84:4–6

When we lived in Boston we were once invited to visit the home of a couple who were part of our parish. They, a struggling and somewhat countercultural twosome with English roots and their two small children, were the owners of—I cannot give it any other name—an ancient tenement building in Dorchester, a blighted municipality huddled in the shadow of the urban congestion of greater Boston. We arrived in the late afternoon on a chilly Sunday in spring. Their flat, they had informed us, was on the fourth level. We stood unproductively pressing their doorbell and kicking aside the litter of peeling paint chips in the dim vestibule for some minutes before we decided to look around back of the building to see if there was another entrance. Slipping through the narrow corridor of space that separated their building from the closely tucked structure next door, we emerged into the area that was, if you stretch the limits of the term, their backyard. There we found all four of our friends vigorously working away on a tiny plot of ground bordered by a dilapidated wire fencing that unsuccessfully delineated their yard from the garbage cans,

172

dissected motorcycles, and waving lines of laundry that spewed from the surrounding tenements.

The husband beamed at us from his place atop a mound of filtered soil. At his side a growing pile of rocks showed the results of many hours spent sifting with a wire frame. Their two-year-old son was deep in the muck of a turned flower bed, thick from head to toe to trowel with the fruits of his gardening labors, his little sister crawled after him delighting in the clods flung from her brother's trowel. The wife greeted us eagerly and proceeded to take us on a tour of their "land." Raised beds, painstakingly urged from this tiny bit of dirt that had survived the overlay of city concrete, brick, steel, and plaster, yielded strawberries, asparagus, beans, peas, onions, root vegetables of various kinds, herbs, and an icing of colorful and ecologically correct flowers. The garden's mistress spoke enthusiastically about manures, rotating crops, planting seasons, organic control of pests. As she commented on the quality of the Dorchester soil, she kept speaking about their "land."

My three children enthusiastically joined in the digging and sifting, the girls heedless of the white tights and patent leather shoes they had insisted on wearing. I, whose experience with like discussions previously had occurred when standing on the edge of a vast acreage of a Montana ranch or strolling within the comfortable rich loamed expanse of a suburban half-acre, was bemused. The whole event was mildly surreal, like something out of a Fellini movie where reality warps slowly into a scene that stretches the categories to which we are accustomed. The wonderful strangeness of the afternoon was enhanced when our friends finally took us up the rotting back staircase into their home. The interior showed heroic efforts to rescue a collapsing structure with few resources but hands and time and the most rudimentary of materials. Most wonderful of all was an elegant and technologically sophisticated telescope given to them by a friend which we were going to enjoy when the day drew to a close. When the sky was finally dark enough (if one can say it is ever dark enough for a telescope in the middle of the artificial glow from a big city), they brought the large telescope out. Where were we going to view the sky, I wondered, peering out the windows into the windows of the adjacent apartments. They took us out onto their back porch, a questionable thin lip of boards with a railing around it that overlooked the garden (and the garbage cans and motorcycle remains). Carefully placing the telescope at one far corner of the porch and pointing it back toward their building so that its eye focused up into the thin strip of sky that peeked above the roof line of the neighboring building, we could crouch down, with our backs leaning against the railing and peer into a tiny fragment of the night sky. Our friends were full of stories of what the astronomical projections were for this time of year and of the astral phenomena they had seen in the past.

My thoughts strayed to a time when an astronomer friend had taken me to the top of Mt. Wilson where scientists come to view the expanse of the universe through the powerful lenses of a sophisticated planetarium. I thought of the reckless fertility of the agricultural lands in the central valley of California with endless acres of produce and of the dome of the sky that stretches from far horizon to far horizon over the plains of the Midwest. And I loved this family who loved their land, such as it was, and who tended and cherished it; and I loved these people who were compelled to look, despite formidable odds, with awe into the depths of the sky spread above them. I loved these people who had made of the wilderness a place of springs.

The gospel that we as Christians proclaim to be the good news is a gospel of peace. From the Lucan infancy narratives in which hosts of angels fill the night sky and announce peace to all people to the post-Resurrection appearances in John in which Jesus reveals himself to his joyful disciples with the greeting "Peace be with you," peace is an integral part of the scriptural message. Even before the birth of Jesus, peace was part of the messianic longing of Israel, a yearning expressed in the canticle of Zachariah, father of John the Baptist:

Blessed be the Lord, the God of Israel for he has visited his people, he has come to their rescue and he has raised up for us a power for Salvation in the House of his Servant David. . . . The tender mercy of God . . . will bring the rising sun to visit us, to give light to those who live in darkness and the shadow of death and to guide our feet into the way of peace. (Luke 1:68–69, 78–79)

This peace promised in the new covenant is both something we long for, yet something we do not have. Peace is conferred as a sign of the Spirit which lives and acts in the body of the Church. It is a gift, a quality of presence intrinsic to our full humanity but is also something that passes our understanding.

For centuries our spiritual heritage has spoken of this gospel imperative of peace as a sort of quality of calm or supernatural indifference that is possessed by the saints. Legends abound of this or that ascetic sailing through the most tumultuous seas of opposition with a faith unruffled and serene. This equation of peace and indifference or detachment has a long history. It is rooted in a specific philosophical synthesis that identifies spiritual growth with a lessening of the "passions" and which places the crown of perfection on the head of one who has achieved a state of passionlessness (*apatheia*). Peace, in this context, is an inner quality cultivated chiefly for the individual's spiritual integrity.

But peace has different meanings for us today. In an era in which unprecedented arsenals of lethal weapons stand poised on all points of our globe ostensibly to deter the aggression of competing nation-states, peace is most obviously a question of war and peace or the management of international conflict.

In the past decade most of the Christian denominations in the United States have issued public position statements on the morality of our present postures of defense and the proliferation of nuclear weaponry whose capabilities for global destruction render obsolete our cherished notions of how we as peoples of varying political, economic, and cultural persuasions go about coexisting together on the earth.[1] The U.S. Catholic bishops pastoral letter on this subject, *The Challenge of Peace*, issued in 1983, speaks clearly of the imperative all Christians have to closely consider the questions of war and peace in light of their faith.

The Challenge of Peace also goes beyond the international arena and invites the Church to consider peace in even broader terms. "Peacemaking is not an optional commitment," it states. Peacemaking is integral to a life lived in response to the gospel. The document encourages all to see peace not only in terms of foreign or domestic policy but in terms of a conversion of heart.

What does being a peacemaker mean? In the marketplace, in the classroom, in the family? What are the skills, the attitudes, the disciplines that can encourage peace, resolve conflict, disarm violence? More deeply even than that: What are the qualities of heart that we must realize so that peace can be a condition of being that offers an alternative to the violence that surrounds us on all sides?

Peacemaking in the Family

Peacemaking is a call to be responded to in the Christian family.[2] There are several levels on which the efforts to learn the arts of peacemaking must take place. First, there are the larger structural issues of justice and "right relationship" that predispose a family to become a fertile plot out of which peace might grow. We know of these structural issues backhandedly through studies done on domestic violence. There are several identifiable factors that in themselves contribute to the incipient violence in families. They are first, social isolation. When families are estranged from a network of supportive relationships, they are likely to exhibit signs of violence. With the high incidence of social mobility separating relatives and creating an ever-transient population, architectural practices that create bedroom communities effectively separating neighbor from neighbor, the demise of the traditional neighborhood, patterns of work and leisure that divide up the family, it is little wonder that the violence engendered by isolation rises to the surface of our national life. The human person is made for community, made to grow from and enrich a network of concern that is best built over a long time and sustained by intimate contact.

Second, violent families tend to be characterized by rigid sex-role stereotyping. Any relationship built on a pattern of dominance and subordination will breed hostility and violence that most likely will be expressed covertly. Similarly, violence is bred in families where there are extreme inequities of power, where the natural authority of those who lead and guide is exercised not to empower others but to control and manipulate. Finally, in violent families poor communication is the norm. When each individual does not find it possible for his or her unique voice to be heard within the family system, violence (expressed physically or otherwise) is often the result.

These are some underlying social factors that inhibit the spirit of peace from dwelling within a family. Beyond the construction of a healthy system, peacemaking in the family is an active process and involves learning new modes of human interaction that seek to diffuse conflict. Both Pax Christi, the international peace organization and the Parenting for Peace and Justice network within the Roman communion have studied the active arts of peacemaking and continue to publish literature and provide audio, video, and live programs about their work.

There are many things families can do to make a peaceful environment by taking the time and making the commitment. They can learn skills in nonviolent communication, really listen to one another, learn to phrase their talk in ways that are not confrontational or accusing but that invite dialogue. They can establish family meetings in which decision-making within the domestic church is shared. They can learn negotiation skills and allow their children to resolve their own conflicts, acting as models rather than as arbiters. Families can remember that gestures of touch (the family hug, resting on each other's arms, being carried and protected) are disarming and healing as well as affirming and are part of the art of peacemaking.

Alongside these gestures, the power of forgiveness stands chief in the peacemaker's repertoire. To be able to recognize and admit one's mistakes as parent or child or in-law; to seek to reconcile when there is estrangement; to heal the broken bonds of intimacy by allowing the self to become vulnerable enough to genuinely forgive and seek forgiveness: These are traits of the peacemaker.

Beyond these acts of peace are the active jobs of parenting that challenge the violence mirrored in society by discussing and eliminating media depictions of violence in all its forms. Then there is the job of nurturing the family imagination for peace, providing alternative models of relationships for the violent ones that dominate our culture's visual and mental fields. In all these ways parents act to create ways of being that make them peacemakers and teach their children about what they might do to become peacemakers themselves.

Teachers of Peace

I sometimes wonder if my struggle to be peacemaker has had any effect at all on my children. It is, after all, the family arena in which I find my capacity for rigidity and incipient violence most exposed. If "peace in the family" equates with polite, well-mannered children who exhibit no signs of sibling rivalry and the ability to resolve skillfully all emergent conflicts, my household cannot qualify. My suspicion is that enhanced managerial skills would take me as close to that "peaceful" family goal as do my efforts at peacemaking.

Yet we do function as models for our children, and I am often surprised by the ways in which mine have absorbed the alternative vision that both my husband and I seek to live in the mainstream of a society which little cherishes Christian values.

This last springtime my husband was filled with a desire to do something about a pile of limbs and logs that lay at the far end of our garden. One Saturday, after a particularly frustrating week at the office, he decided to rent a chainsaw and go to work on the fallen tree debris. He wanted to saw something and relished the thought of bearing down on that wood with fervor. Catharsis— that was what was needed. The logs would provide it. But the announcement of his impending plans provoked cries of alarm from our two girls. Those fallen logs had been their fairyland. They had set up games there. There was no other "secret place" in our yard for them to play. This was their sacred place (yes, they called it that). He *could not* cut the logs.

He was headed in too straight a line to pay much attention to them. "The logs are an eyesore!" he declared and set off to the equipment rental store for the chainsaw. The girls were not to be dissuaded. "He can't do that to our fairyland," they wailed in tears. The younger became belligerent, "I'll put on war paint and beat him up when he gets home!" she fumed. Her older sister had another plan. "No," she stated, "We will stage a nonviolent demonstration. We will protest the injustice of what he is doing!"

They ran off into the house. I was in the garden pulling weeds from the vegetable patch and decided to remain neutral and just observe what happened. Pretty soon they came out again. With them now was their little brother. Each was wearing a tee shirt on which the words "Save the Logs" had been printed in crayola on front and back. They were carrying cardboard signs scotch-taped onto twigs on which were scrawled these slogans: "Save Nature—Leave the Logs Alone," "Nature Knows Best," "Nature Did It First," "If *God* Put Them Here, *God* Must Want Them Here," "Please Reconsider," "Decide on Compromise." My middle daughter (who was just learning to read and write) held the sign she had made herself: "No. No. No. No. No. No. No. No. No."

They sat down on the logs and planned their strategy. "We must be calm and firm," my eldest instructed the demonstrators. "We must appeal to his conscience." She began to teach them the song she had written for the occasion:

> [Refrain]   "Please reconsider. This is nature at its best.
> Save Nature, Save Nature."

[Verse 1]   "Don't act like a big corporation. Please
understand. We'll try to make a
compromise. We'll help you through."

[Refrain]   "Please reconsider . . . "

[Verse 2]   "If God didn't want it there then why is it
there?
Please understand. Save Nature."

[Refrain]   "Please reconsider . . . "

They practiced diligently. They practiced singing "We Shall
Overcome." Then came a failure of nerve. The waiting was getting tedious. "He won't pay any attention." "He'll just do what
he wants." Then came what to my ears sounded like a succinct
analysis of the temptations of power and authority. "He'll just say
this is *his*. He *owns* it and can do what he wants with it." "But
what about us? Maybe we don't own it but we have a right to say
what's done to it!"

They were almost giving up when the car rolled into the driveway. They galvanized for action. Up went their signs. Little bodies
were seated indignantly between their sacred space and the ad-
vancing chainsaw. "We shall overcome. We shall overcome," they
quavered. My husband, in a mood to brook no opposition, arrived at the tiny demonstration. They began their song, "Please
reconsider." I'm not sure he was amused. He needed to saw something. Those eyesore logs had been grating at him all winter. He
had just spent twenty dollars renting a chainsaw to get rid of
them.

They offered him a compromise. He could saw the log near the
mulberry tree. But he had to leave alone the circle of logs they
had designated as their space. I cannot claim that this demonstration ended in a triumphant celebration of the power of nonviolent resistance, but it did save the logs. Daddy, irked, sawed away
at the lone log by the mulberry, too frustrated to be gracious or
charmed by their witness. Yet he sawed only the one log and a
large pile of tree branches. The wood turned out to be so hard

that the sawing of just that amount of kindling took him all afternoon and produced the physical catharsis he needed. The girls were not sufficiently aware of their "victory." They were so worn out and ready to be on to other things by that time that I'm not sure they savored the fruits of their labors. I did.

I savored the fact that somewhere in their vision of what the world can be is a sense that there are alternatives to the way things are generally done. Somehow they know that the voices of the small and the dispossessed must rightfully be heard. Somehow they know that to appeal to conscience, to speak truth, to witness to that in action is a legitimate response to the "evils" of the world.

Blessed Are the Peacemakers

Above and beyond the active efforts in conflict resolution and nonviolent resistance that create the opportunity for peace in the family, there is the question of peace as a quality of heart. In my perception I see these two as interrelated but not identical. The active efforts toward establishing a nonviolent environment seem to me to be very much like the "straightening of the path" we are called to do by John the Baptist in Advent. He is the messenger, the essential voice crying out in the wilderness that we must repent, get ready, reform our ways. The bringer of peace is yet to come. Peace comes as a gift, as the touch of the divine that enters so fully into human nature that the two, human and divine, are intimately bound.

This peace is a quality of heart. Yet I cannot speak of it using the somewhat static language of our spiritual tradition: peace as indifference or passionlessness or as the supernatural ability to be unmoved by what would normally move one. I would begin to describe it rather differently. I would describe it as the heart of a child that knows both its dependence on and identity with its loving parent, a child who has been willing to undergo the radical conversion necessary for its heart to be thus transformed. This is what God has promised us through the prophets—that we shall be God's people, that God will be our God. We will be set free, we shall be taken from among the nations, gathered in from foreign lands. A new Spirit will be placed within us. Our hearts of stone will be taken away. Instead we will tenderly be given hearts made of flesh—hearts capable of genuine love, for God and each other. Hearts such as these are deeply blessed, rightly named as hearts of the children of God. They are hearts that bear imprinted on them the gospel of the Son of God—the Prince of Peace—who is brother to us all. Blessed are the peacemakers for they shall be called children of God.

I would like to share with you my own inner struggles to open my life enough to the enspiriting presence of God to enter me and begin to claim and reshape my heart. The arena of conversion is among the intimate relationships of my own family. It is there that I have discovered, not my capacity for peacemaking, but my capacity for violence. It is in the encounters with those who are closest and dearest to me that I have had revealed to me my own very real limitations, my rigidity, my anger, my incapacity to love.

I have always wanted to be peaceful with my family. I am not capable of that much of the time. Especially after the birth of my third child, I felt that all the neat ways I had of coping with my life fell apart. I've always been high-strung but suddenly it was all beyond me and I found myself screaming at people a lot and being constantly irritated at my older children who never seemed to stay in line. I felt like a failure. And what was worse, I felt guilty about not being able to hold it all together.

In fact, it was sort of cathartic to have to admit that I couldn't do everything, that I really *needed* God, that I wanted to be peacemaker, but was incapable of being so. That was the starting point of the conversion—the dual recognition that my own limits were very real and not about to go away and that this recognition was probably in some odd way blessed. I was stuck with myself like this for the duration.

I began to sense that my previous motives for wanting to be a peacemaker were shallow. Probably I had been working out of the "nice mom" syndrome. I mean, aren't moms always nice? That's what I wanted it to look like to the world (and myself). And I guess for a long time that that person lulled me into a false peaceful state. Peace equalled not rocking the boat or not making a fuss or keeping the lid on all things unseemly. (How many women have spent lifetimes maintaining this kind of false peace—even to the extent of being codependent on some really violent patterns of family behavior—all in the name of peace?)

But true peace cannot be identified with simply the absence of conflict. True peace is something else, it is a state of being. Anger is not antithetical to peace. In fact, sometimes a rightful outrage is necessary to redress situations of injustice so that the conditions of true peace might be met. There is an adage that goes, "If you want peace, work for justice." This is true in the family. Peace does not exist because everyone simply looks the other way when relationships are skewed or hurtful. No. We must struggle creatively with one another to come into right relationship. This just way of being together creates a climate for the arrival of the gift of peace.

So I had to look at my own capacity for violence. As I looked long and hard, I could see that it was only a matter of degrees that separated my incipient violence from the terrible, even criminal violence, of many families. Given an unbearable combination of stressful pressures, no doubt I could be provoked to unthinkable extremes.

The next step after this recognition was not only acceptance of my own lack of peacefulness but the ability to love it. I began to see clearly what God sees all along—that we are all blessed and broken, gifted and incapable at the same time. But God's wondrous love embraces all of it. Not only did I learn to let God love the unlovable parts of myself—I even began to love them, to try and be tender and patient with my own shortcomings the same way I try to be gentle with the immaturities of my own kids. My heart began to gentle a bit, to be less unforgiving of myself, more open to receiving the mixed blessing and brokenness of those around me. For to pull back in horror at your own violence keeps you chained inside yourself and invulnerable. No, none of us has it "all together." We need new hearts, we need each other, we need God. We need to know our own needfulness, need to have hearts willing to say, "I am not enough."

Hearts such as these become hearts that are open, willing to be entered and filled, even to overflowing. These needful hearts can become vessels for the fuller life of God that wants to come and live in us but has difficulty because our hearts are so often closed.

I already knew something about this quality of heart from my relationship with my children. How much of my own heart has been opened by them, willing to rejoice and to suffer with another, willing to be taken where I myself might not choose to go. I felt that I was asked to make the best qualities of both a mother and a child live in my own heart. The chief characteristic of such a heart is its flexibility. It can be stretched and shaped by the loves that enter it.

Yet what I knew of a mother's flexible heart did not necessarily speak to me of peace. To be open in such expanse is to be vulnerable to many conflicting elements, even to let the heart be torn by what enters it. No, peace did not mean absence of conflict. But where was peace in the jumble of experience and emotion that enters an unguarded heart? Gradually I began to see that there was a deep kind of loving in such a heart that had been shown to me in the heart of Jesus, God's firstborn child.

Jesus' love allowed all human experience to enter deeply into him. His heart welcomed the giftedness of all, but did not reject the brokenness either. *All* that was in the human heart entered into him. All the deepest hope, the most cherished vision of humankind found its consummation in him. Yet all that acts to daunt hope, to destroy vision was drawn to him as well. His heart became the forge within which darkness and light met. His response was not to "resolve" the conflict, but to become a place of transformation. He stood at a point of supreme tension in the universe. His love was so expansive that all the evil that confronted him did not transform him into itself. He did not give back in kind what was dealt out to him. Neither did he experience himself as the rightful victim of the evil that befell him. There was always in him the foundational knowledge of himself as blessed child of God, inheritor of a dignity and worth that should merit justice and love. His knowing heart became a place where that deep knowledge in fact disarmed and transformed evil. Not without immense pain. But that receptive heart embraced the ambiguity of human experience in its depth where it knew integrity and the nature of the true self. His heart became a place of transformation where love indeed was stronger than death, where the love of others seen in the refusal to treat them as he had been treated and the love of knowing himself as child of God, transformed sin and death into new life.

This was the heart of the firstborn of God. This was the heart that nonviolently resisted all that would warp and crush the image of God in creation. This truly was the peacemaker's heart. "Peace be with you. My peace I give you" (John 14:27).

Peace is a gift of the Spirit for which we prepare. We straighten the roads of our hearts so that by our actions and our learning the arts of nonviolence we can be ready when the gift is sent. We feel the Spirit touch us when we are able to truly know ourselves and others as beloved children of one God. We breathe the Spirit when we are filled with wonder at what is. We let the Spirit pass through us when we become places of transformation, when the dark night of holding together the irreconcilable tensions of our lives gives way to some new constellation, when out of chaos creation comes.

Our hearts are Spirit-filled not when they can figure everything out or neatly dispose of parts of experience. Our hearts are the hearts of children of God when they love expansively enough to trust the contradictions, the opposition, the vast variety that we encounter in our world. We have the Spirit of peace when we have hearts that break and tear with suffering and exult with the rapture that surrounds us. Such hearts animated by the divine life love so deeply that neither pain nor bitter disillusionment can negate that trust. Such hearts have touched the ground of the universe and know that it is love.

·13·

In any part of the country where the porch is still part of the architectural language of homes, you will find people sitting. Often alone, sometimes in groups of two or three, sometimes in larger numbers, people congregate on the porch. In our own neighborhood the house next door has a porch of classic design that faces majestically out to the street and is set off from the passing front traffic by two steps yet is easily accessible from the sidewalk by way of an inviting path. There the neighborhood tends to gather. On a sticky hot summer afternoon the husband or wife will be discovered sitting on the porch in a state of quiet repose. Soon a neighbor, recovering from the labors of weed-pulling will gravitate toward them and find himself seated sipping iced tea. A young mother from across the street might end up there for a few restful minutes, bringing the bottle of nail polish that she hopes to use during the baby's nap. Often that porch is a playtime haven for the dozen or so preschool children who streak back and forth between the neighborhood yards in a giggly and barefooted cluster. Sometimes the porch serves as the theater for the drama of teenage life that goes on within the house. The porch will suddenly sport a blaring radio and the restless, casually draped bodies of local high school friends hanging from the railings and cascading down the front steps. More often than not, however, the porch is the seating place for one person alone. It becomes a hermit space. There lengthy discourse is unnecessary. There it is all right to just look and listen. There silence is already fulsome and need not be artificially filled.

In neighborhoods where the porch is nonexistent, the front stoop of the row house or apartment complex often becomes the place of sitting. Or, in urban areas where the stoop is unused, porchlike activity will often take place on the tree-sheltered bench of a city park. All these spaces share in being natural areas of contemplative awareness, sitting spaces where agendas are suspended, where the way to be is to be given over to the sweet, unhurried perception of what is. They are sacred spaces that celebrate the *is-ness* of things.

From the porch one observes the simple rhythms of daily life: the neighbor setting out the garbage in the early morning, the woman from the next street who regularly walks her little dog just after suppertime, the school-age boys exercising prowess in bicycling, the elderly widow receiving a rare visit from an in-law, the businesslike drivers of passing cars whose faces mirror their intent to get where they are going.

On the porch one hears the sounds that surround us—the worried chirping of jays hovering over a nest, the cries of the waking baby across the street, the approaching bell of the ice cream man's truck, the distant sirens from the city, the sounds of the neighborhood dogs whose resonant barks carry airborne canine conversations well over the barriers of fenced-in yards.

Seated upon the porch one finds it unnecessary to comment upon or analyze what one sees and hears. It is enough that it is. Being is not something to be taken for granted nor overlooked, but something to be breathed in and celebrated with sweet contentment and a grateful heart. The porch is the home's sacred space of contemplation, the structural articulation of the home's most treasured and earnest secret. The porch speaks mutely all that we cannot say, but that we nonetheless know to be truest about our lives.

The *Is-ness* of Things

I visited Polonnaruwa [Ceylon] on Monday. . . . A low
outcrop of rock, with a cave cut into it, and beside the cave
a big seated Buddha on the left, a reclining Buddha on the
right, and Ananda, I guess, standing by. . . . I am able to
approach the [carved] Buddhas barefoot and undisturbed,
my feet in wet grass, wet sand. Then the silence of the
extraordinary faces . . . Filled with every possibility,
questioning nothing, knowing everything, rejecting
nothing, . . . Looking at these figures I was suddenly almost
forcibly, jerked clean out of the habitual half-tied vision of
things and an inner clearness, clarity, as if exploding from
the rocks themselves, became evident and obvious. The
queer *evidence* of the reclining figure . . . the thing about all
this is that there is no puzzle, no problem and really no
"mystery." All problems are resolved and everything is
clear, simply because what matters is clear. The rock, all
matter, all life is charged with dharmakaya. . . . everything
is emptiness and everything is compassion. . . . I know and
have seen what I was obscurely looking for. . . . It says
everything; it can afford to be silent, unnoticed,
undiscovered. It does not need to be discovered. It is we . . .
who need to discover it.

The Asian Journal of Thomas Merton

We frequently take a trip from our home in Omaha, Nebraska
to Manhattan, Kansas, where my mother-in-law lives. To make
the north-south journey we have to travel close to two hundred
miles of road. Only about twenty of those miles are interstate
highway. The rest are country roads which, although they form

the major arteries of travel, are two lanes at most. The scenery basically consists of agricultural or pasture land. Anticipated landmarks along the way are the llama farms alongside the road in Tecumseh and the "Hilltop Cafe," a one-room diner (not on a hill or even on a rise) that boasts four booths and a counter with about six of those wonderful stools that children love to spin. The special of the day is often a "gizzard basket" served with fries. We also look forward to whizzing by the tiny town of Burchard that advertises itself as the birthplace of Harold Lloyd.

North-south travel in this part of our nation is very light. Once we leave the Omaha area we can anticipate traveling for up to an hour without seeing another vehicle. When we do, it is likely to be a tractor creeping slowly through the fields. Cities are nonexistent, but there are a dozen or so minuscule communities that serve as gathering space for the local inhabitants, most of whom farm or raise livestock. So many of these communities are virtually ghost towns. Once thriving agricultural centers, they have succumbed as the American family farm has become a disappearing species. Particularly poignant is Frankfort, Nebraska, whose downtown spans about four city blocks. Half of the stores are now vacant, an unused grain elevator spreads a shadow over its streets. There is still a storefront that has the words "Frankfort Public Library" stenciled on the window and a bar and sandwich shop called Helen's where you can buy gum and where the local men in overalls trade stories over a beer in the late afternoon.

Driving through the deserted streets of Frankfort on a recent trip, we passed by an elderly gentleman sitting on his porch in the gathering twilight. His reverie was complete. As our lone car drove slowly by our middle daughter asked, "What's he doing out there?" My husband quipped back, "Watching the car go by." We chuckled at his response but knew this was not the true one. The elderly gentleman was doing what sitters-on-porches are really doing—contemplating the *is-ness* of things.

Sometimes I think that the deepest meaning of family life consists in our learning something of what that porch-sitting gentleman was doing. Living in that complex, ever-fluctuating network of familial relationships—having one's heart filled and emptied, made generous yet twisted tight in pain beyond belief, grappling with self and other—sometimes feels like being in the grip of a cyclone. Yet at the center of every cyclone there is a quiet stillness. We know that quiet in family when we tiptoe into the darkened room of a sleeping infant. We know it when we open the drawer of an unused desk and come upon the handkerchief or rosary that was in the constant keeping of a deceased grandmother. We know it when we wait expectantly in the crowd outside the airline gate for an absent family member to peek his or her head out of an arriving airplane door. We know it when we ritually press into our wallets the recent school photos of our children or grandchildren. We know it when we smell the aroma of Thanksgiving turkey or the perfume of homebaked bread kneaded by familiar hands.

There is a quality of stillness at the heart of the most hectic of families, an inexplicable knowing that surpasses our ability to give it form in words. The wholeness of what we are, the myriad experiences of inhabiting, of love, hurt, betrayal, reconciliation, welcome, loss, sometimes come together in a moment of simple seeing.

My eldest daughter spoke it underneath her words recently when the sad death of one of our cat's newborn kittens plunged her into an experience of grief. I heard her cry for more than one small cat and cry out her realization that dying was part of life, that everyone she now loved—parents, grandparents, friends— could be and would sometime be taken away. She wept inconsolably. Yet the next day she came up to me and confided that she had heard before that a house was not a home until it had a birth, a death, and a wedding in it. Now our house had within it both birth and death. Our house was well on its way to becoming a home.

People of the Earth

Our sense of the is-ness of things is in part, I think, rooted in our knowledge of ourselves as people of the earth. Most of us, urban dwellers that we are, have become estranged from this way of knowing. At least one recent Christian critic of the unprecedented technological changes that characterize modern society points out the profound psychic and spiritual implications of such change: how for instance, our ability (through the invention of the electric light) to deny and destroy darkness has impoverished our capacity to deal creatively with our own darkness and to "read" the images of light and dark so foundational to our Christian faith.[1]

Certainly, early Christian monastic practice was undergirded by an ethos of earth-belonging that is not well appreciated. The obligatory prayer of the community occurred in rhythm with the rising, progress, and setting of the sun. The canonical hours were said seven times daily and, in an age in which time was not dictated by the clock, those hours were determined by the fluctuations in the solar realm, not by a strict chronological division. Matins was at dawn. Vespers at dusk. In the summer the days were genuinely longer. One rose early and went to bed late with the sun. In winter one's day was correspondingly short.

In the *Rule of St. Benedict* (that sixth-century synthesis of existent monastic practice that by the ninth century became the normative rule for virtually all European monastic establishments), not only was time measured by the rhythms of the earth, but manual work and the production of food from the land was part of the way of life. The monks' prayer was not confined by liturgical outlines but spread out into the daily occupations of life.

There is a natural contemplative awareness of the is-ness of things among people who live in a close relationship to the earth. Any farmer who has lovingly prepared and worked the soil knows the numinousness of the ecosystem of which we are one part. Earth, water, seed, and air become the intuitive knowledge of identity and the context of meaning-making. I have been told by friends who have ministered extensively in rural areas that the true place of prayer and the practice of the presence of God is not in the pew but on the seat of the tractor.

Even urban gardeners have recovered their roots in the earth. An article in a recent issue of *Organic Gardening* spoke of this in eloquent terms:

> For those who live off the land, their plot is the center of creation. Beyond its boundaries is another world populated by hired laborers and tax collectors, merchants and consumers. Being able to rest in the shade of a sycamore or a walnut tree planted by grandparents or great-grandparents gives a sense of rootedness no city can offer.
>
> Nevertheless, no new homeowner anxiously placing petunia seedlings in a tiny townhouse yard starts from scratch. Coded in our genes are the instincts for planting and cultivation. It is surprisingly easy to relearn how to wield a spade, a hoe, a rake. Even for the rankest beginner, to do yard work is to go back to the land. Launching a mixed border or a vegetable patch is always a return, a reunion and, sometimes, a reconciliation.
>
> Improving soil is self-improvement. It is to be attuned to the cycle of decline and growth; to participate in the dialectic of creation, preservation and dissolution; to bring together parts of a shattered whole. Whether burying garbage directly in the soil or spreading the contents of a compost pile, it is intoxicating to watch stiff red clay (Adam was shaped from it) or pale lifeless sand (mortar holding buildings together is made with it) turn into rich soil dark with nutrients.
>
> Desert dwellers sense brooding spirits in the miracle of an oasis. In the Bible, it is often by a well that conflict and alliance, war and marriage are sealed. And it is on a blood-soaked battlefield that the grass is the greenest and the grain is the fattest.
>
> Helping a seed to sprout, flower and fruit is trafficking with the elements. Reaping one good harvest after another is practicing magic.
>
> Alienation means having lost connection with the soil. It is a state of indifference to how food is grown and how beauty is born out of petal and leaf. Being alienated means having forgotten to be grateful for the largess of the good earth.

According to the government and the documents it issues, a person owns a piece of land. But, in reality, the land owns the person; he or she is its tenant. Land is a demanding mistress. She requires digging and irrigation, care and replenishment. She needs to be changed from wheat field to pasture and from pasture to vegetables or to flowers. Of all possessions, land is the most precious and the hardest to part with; to give up land seems to mean giving up life.[2]

People of the earth. Attuned to the wisdom of life-giving humus, the patience of rocks, the dignity of trees and the essential contribution of each creeping-crawling thing, we come to know something of the divine milieu of which we are a part. Teilhard de Chardin has had, of Christians, perhaps the most lyrical voice to proclaim the spiritual power of matter. Teilhard speaks of the presence of God in the world as source and consummation of the entire world and as its process of becoming. For him, the universe itself is a hymn to the Creator.

Family spirituality is rooted in the earth—in the interpenetration of flesh, the creation of flesh from flesh, in the fluids of milk, semen, urine, sweat and tears, in the hard labors of our hands. It is there—in the very matter of which we are formed— that the divine can be discerned.

Giving Thanks

To grasp in fullness the simple mystery of being that lies behind our many experiences is to know the is-ness of things. There are times given to us in family life when that mystery is glimpsed. Moments of birth and death give us our most heightened experiences. But all moments are potential opportunities to touch the fullness of who we are. The difficulty is that it is so hard for everyone in a family to sit still long enough for a contemplative repose to be achieved. If sitting still is not something you or your family do very well, there is another way to grasp the mystery. The key is giving thanks.

We once took a Maine vacation. It was late in the summer and
for many months we had not been out of the city of Cambridge
where we lived because of the impending birth, birth, and early
infancy of our third child. All of us desperately needed a vacation. We had heard so much about the beauties of the northeast-
ern coastline and wanted to see something of them. Strapped for
money, and stealing precious time off from work, we decided to
take our vacation. A young artist who owned a house on Penob-
scot Bay had advertised in a local paper that she was looking for
renters for ten days while she attended an art institute. The price
was right and we jumped at the opportunity. Early one morning
we set off on the long trek northward, planning to arrive at our
destination (with the many requisite stops) by evening. Although I
have a nearly nonexistent faith in our family's ability to travel
with any sort of dignity and decorum, I had done all I could to
anticipate any emergency.

Everything seemed ideal for about a half an hour. Then our
two-year-old daughter vomited her breakfast all over the back-
seat. That set the tone for the remainder of the trip. We discovered that the baby, just a few months old, was content sitting in
his car seat while he was sleeping but howled when strapped in it
awake. I think he thought we were trying to get him to sleep
again. He had never been for a long drive in the car. Needless to
say, he slept little and howled most of the way. We stopped frequently so I could nurse him and so that the girls could run
around for a bit, but he began to cry each time we started up
again. The girls began to fight. They bickered, teased, and
shrieked. All of our nerves were frayed.

By the time we arrived at our lodgings, it was late and dark. I
wanted nothing more than to sink into the oblivion of bed, but
the discovery of our new living space perked the kids up and they
began streaking around joyously. The place, we discovered, was
what I shall call funky. Now I have a high tolerance for funky but
this place was the other side of funky where adjectives like
"decrepit" or "trashed" come to the lips. But we were there and

eventually all sank into sleep. My urgently pleaded nighttime prayer was that everyone would sleep in just a little later in the morning. I, still depleted from an arduous birth and bleary-eyed from interrupted nights, needed rest most of all.

As fate would have it, the tiny bed alcove into which the children and I eventually piled (due to the musical beds effect that always seems to occur in a new place) had two enormous unshaded and unshuttered windows that faced the east. The glorious radiance of the sun streamed in on us about four or five hours after we had all finally fallen asleep.

My eldest daughter woke with the sun. She was radiant with anticipation. "The beach! The beach!" She shouted at full voice, "Let's go down to the beach!" I tried to hush her but she woke our other daughter who immediately began to cry. She wanted a bottle, she wailed. She was grumpy with sleeplessness. I tried to hush them both and stumbled around trying to find a bottle among the rubble of the suitcases that had been plopped in the doorway the night before. Then I couldn't find the juice. All the commotion startled the baby who began to cry. Our middle daughter, still green-eyed and jealous of the usurping sibling, began to move menacingly toward the baby. My eldest continued to insist at full voice that she wanted to go to the beach—NOW! I tried to explain that the waterfront was a good half mile down the hill from the house and that we were not ready yet to go out of doors. She became very angry and declared she was GOING TO GO OUT, NOW! I said she was not. She started to storm out but stepped in a pool of pee that had formed beneath her sister who, still weeping, had pulled off the disposable diaper she was wearing. Now the two girls begin to scream at each other, adding their howls to the wails of the baby. I managed to find the juice and the bottle but came back into the room just in time to see my bare-bottomed daughter lunge at the baby and bite his leg. Pulling her off of him, I picked him up, gave her the bottle and tried to settle him down to nurse. It was impossible. I was close to screaming myself and so limp with exhaustion from the short night that I was close to tears. With gritted teeth, I realized that my husband was sleeping through all of this, tucked in his sleeping bag neatly out of earshot in the living room.

My eldest daughter was by now hysterical, ranting on about running down to the seashore alone in her nightclothes. Frantic and pushed beyond control, I leapt up and shook her fiercely by the shoulders. "You've hurt me," she screamed in a shocked voice. Had I? I wondered. Confused, furious, remorseful, I somehow gathered up all three wailing children, hauled them into the living room and dumped them on the inert body of my sleeping spouse. Then I ran outdoors into the low lying fog of the Maine morning, hurled my nightgowned self onto the stump of a fallen tree and cried.

When I returned to the house, things had calmed down. But my heart was agitated and remained so for much of the day. How was I going to negotiate *three* children? Would we never make a graceful adjustment to one more? Why was this anticipated special time so marred by ill spirits and anger? How could I have shaken her so hard? What kind of lousy mom was I anyway? Where *was* God in all this? What kind of cosmic joke was this family life? Why didn't anyone *help* me? On and on the relentless thoughts went. Late in the morning we all climbed into the car and headed for the nearby town to have lunch and buy provisions for the week (we had spent some time on the beach in the morning). I was sick with exhaustion but stubbornly kept going. I sat in the front seat with my miserable thoughts churning around in my head.

Then, somehow, my mind strayed to a time in graduate school when I had heard a lecture on the religious thoughts of the Danish philosopher Søren Kierkegaard. Kierkegaard, the professor had said, had written a commentary on the biblical phrase, "In all things, give thanks." In it he described giving thanks as a formative act, something enjoined on all Christians not because events naturally elicit from us a spirit of gratitude, but because the act of giving thanks itself changed us and our perceptions.

"In all things give thanks." Impossible, I thought, still reeling from the onslaught of the dawn. Then I heard myself say, somewhat ironically, "Thanks God! Thanks bunches. This is real great!" Then I tried it again, dropping the irony and struggling to find the simple place within which at least the words could be uttered. "Thank you" I said flatly. Then again, "Thank you." Gradually the luxuriant scenery we were passing began to come into consciousness, slowly my fixation on my own exhaustion and anger began to give way. "Thank you," I said. And I felt my heart begin to melt. "Thank you for each of them. Thank you for our aliveness. For our here-ness, for the capacity to cry, to scream, to get angry, for the whole thing. For life, for our silly, petty struggles. For the squirming, impossible mess of it all. Yes, genuinely thank you." And a tender, compassionate love for the is-ness of it all flooded into my heart. All of it. Somehow all deeply blessed. Thank you.

In intervening years I have often forgotten the grace of gratitude, but on occasion I remember, and when I do I learn anew the mysterious power of giving thanks and how it changes me and how it opens in me humor and playfulness and acceptance of what is. For, in fact, all that we have is given. Life itself is a gift. We are the recipients of time, of the gracious earth, of each other's lives. These are given to us. Acquiring the spirit of gratitude serves to heighten our awareness of God's gift, of the is-ness of things.

Notes

Preface

1. St. Jerome, "Against Helvidius: The Perpetual Virginity of Blessed Mary," in *Nicene and Post-Nicene Fathers of the Christian Church*, vol. 6, *St. Jerome: Letters and Select Works* (Grand Rapids, Mich.: Wm. B. Eerdmans, 1954), pp. 344–45.

2. Sharon Parks of Harvard Divinity School has developed this idea in an unpublished paper entitled "Home and Pilgrimage: Spirituality as Nurture toward a Vision of our Planet as a Dwelling Place for the Whole Human Family," which was given for the Ecumenical Institute of Spirituality meeting held in Florida in 1987. In addition, two other recent books utilize the image of home to explore the spiritual life. See Betsy Caprio and Thomas M. Hedberg, S.D.B., *Coming Home: A Handbook for Exploring the Sanctuary Within* (Mahwah, N.J.: Paulist Press, 1986), and Thomas Howard, *Hallowed Be This House* (Wheaton, Ill.: Harold Shaw Pubs., 1978).

Also, Carol Ochs in her book *Women and Spirituality* (Totowa, N.J.: Rowman and Allanheld, 1983) has offered an alternative to the journey metaphor so often employed to describe the spiritual life. She suggests that "the walk" is a more apt image for women whose lives, in the acts of mothering, are less focused on the future goal than the present process of being and being with another.

APPROACH TO THE HOME

1. A succinct treatment of the profile of the American Christian family is found in *A Family Perspective in Church and Society*, by the United States Catholic Conference Commission on Marriage and Family Life (Washington, D.C.: United States Catholic Conference, 1985). For a feminist reevaluation of family issues see the collection of essays *Rethinking the Family: Some Feminist Questions*, ed. Barrie Thorne with Marilyn Yalom (New York: Longman, 1982), and Jane C. Peck, *Self and Family,*

Choices: Guides for Today's Woman Series, vol. 11 (Philadelphia: Westminster, 1984).

2. A number of critiques exist of the context in which the American family attempts to define itself as Christian. Some of the best are Jim and Kathy McGinnis, *Parenting for Peace and Justice* (Maryknoll, N.Y.: Orbis Books, 1981), and John F. Kavanaugh, S.J., *Following Christ in a Consumer Society* (Maryknoll, N.Y.: Orbis Books, 1981).

3. For a feminist critique of this idea of the family as primary nurturer, see Jane Collier et al., "Is There a Family? New Anthropological Views," in *Rethinking the Family*.

4. Etienne Bachelard, *The Poetics of Space* (Boston: Beacon Press, 1969).

5. For a well-done study of the "functional family," see Dolores Curran, *Traits of a Healthy Family* (Minneapolis: Winston Press, 1983).

6. The "already but not yet" phrase was coined by German theologian Wolfhart Pannenberg.

7. See *Familiaris Consortio*, "On the Family," apostolic exhortation of 1981 (Washington, D.C.: United States Catholic Conference, 1982), and Stanley L. Saxton, ed., *The Changing Family: Views from Theology and the Social Sciences in the Light of the Apostolic Exhortation Familiaris Consortio* (Chicago: Loyola University Press, 1983).

8. See especially Mitch and Kathy Finley, *Christian Families in the Real World* (Chicago: Thomas More Press, 1984).

WITHIN

Chapter 1. A Matter of the Heart

1. *The Spiritual Exercises of St. Ignatius,* trans. Louis J. Puhl (Chicago: Loyola University Press, 1951), introductory observations, p. 1.

2. A couple of examples of this genre are Janie Gustafson, *Celibate Passion* (San Francisco: Harper and Row, 1978), and Mary A. Huddleston, ed., *Celibate Loving: Encounter in Three Dimensions* (New York: Paulist Press, 1984).

Chapter 2. A Time for Wonder

1. One lovely book that creatively explores the liturgical life of families is Gertrude Mueller Nelson's *To Dance with God: Family Ritual and Community Celebration* (New York: Paulist Press, 1986). See also Edward Hays, *Prayers for the Domestic Church: A Handbook for Worship in the Home* (Easton, Kans.: Forest of Peace Books, 1979), for a collection of prayers for family occasions whose language is fresh and evocative.

2. *Family Spirituality: The Sacred in the Ordinary,* A Report of the National Association of Catholic Diocesan Family Life Ministers, 1984.

Chapter 3. The Christ-Room
1. Dolores Leckey in her *The Ordinary Way: A Family Spirituality* (New York: Crossroad, 1982) explores the concept of hospitality in the family in relation to the monastic discipline of hospitality that is delineated in the *Rule of St. Benedict*.
2. From *House of Hospitality*, quoted in Dorothy Day, *Meditations*, selected and arranged by Stanley Vishnewski (New York: Paulist Press, 1970), p. 13.
3. Ibid., p. 21.
4. Ibid., p. 40.

Chapter 4. Body of Christ
1. E. V. Wright's "When Father Carves a Duck" is anthologized in *Humorous Poetry for Children*, ed. William Cole (Cleveland: World Publications, 1955).

Chapter 5. A Way That You Know Not
1. Vera A. Krokonko's "The Spiritual Journey of a Single Parent," in *Studies in Formative Spirituality* 7, no. 1 (February 1986), treats this theme. There is a chapter on single parenting in Mitch and Kathy Finley's *Christian Families in the Real World*. One of the few articles I know of about the single person is Francine Cardman's "On Being Single" in *The Wind is Rising: Prayer Ways for Active People*, ed. William Callahan and Francine Cardman (Mt. Rainier, Md.: Quixote Center, February 1978).

DEEPER WITHIN

Chapter 6.
1. Christopher Alexander, Sara Ishikawa, Murray Silverstein, et al., *A Pattern Language* (New York: Oxford University Press, 1977), p. 865.

Male and Female God Created Them
1. Other recent treatments of the spirituality of marriage include Anthony Padovano, *Love and Destiny* (New York: Paulist Press, 1987); Morton T. Kelsey and Barbara Kelsey, *Sacrament of Sexuality* (Warwick, N.Y.: Amity House, 1986); David M. Thomas, *Christian Marriage: A Journey Together* (Wilmington, Del.: Michael Glazier); Michael G. Lawler, *Secular Marriage, Christian Sacrament* (Mystic, Conn.: Twenty-Third Pubns., 1985); George Maloney, Mary Rosseau, and Paul Wilczak, *Embodied in Love* (New York: Crossroad, 1983). On the question of spirituality in ecumenical marriages, see "Mixed Marriages, Helping Interfaith Couples Grow," *Catholic Update* no. 091 (Cincinnati: St. Anthony Messenger Press, 1981). On mutuality from a feminist perspective,

see Beverly Wildung Harrison, "Human Sexuality and Mutuality," in *Christian Feminism*, ed. Judith L. Weidman (San Francisco: Harper and Row, 1984). See also Rosemary Haughton's classic *Theology of Marriage* (Cork, Ireland: Mercier Press) and *The Mystery of Sexuality* (New York: Paulist Press, 1972).

2. Robert Bellah et al., *Habits of the Heart: Individualism and Commitment in American Life* (San Francisco: Harper and Row, 1986).

3. There are several methods of natural family planning taught. Information on the Ovulation Method can be obtained by writing: Pope Paul VI Institute, 6901 Mercy Rd., Omaha, NE 68106.

4. On the issue of the psychology of gender, see especially Carol Gilligan, *In a Different Voice* (Cambridge, Mass.: Harvard University Press, 1982), and Mary F. Belenky et al., *Women's Ways of Knowing: The Development of Self, Voice and Mind* (New York: Basic, 1986).

Chapter 7. In the Circle of a Mother's Arms

1. There is a considerable body of literature on parenting, little of it dealing with the spirituality of that occupation. Notable among books and articles that do attempt to deal with the depth dimensions of parenting are Margaret Hebblethwaite, *Motherhood and God* (San Francisco: Harper and Row, 1984); Dolores Leckey, "Sacred Shelters: Families and Spiritual Empowerment," in *Living with Apocalypse: Spiritual Resources for Social Compassion*, ed. Tilden H. Edwards (Washington, D.C.: Shalem Institute for Spiritual Formation, 1984); and Carol Och, *Women and Spirituality*. Three provocative treatments of mothering from divergent perspectives are Kathryn Rabuzzi, *The Sacred and the Feminine: Toward a Theology of Housework* (New York: Seabury Press, 1982); Sarah Ruddick, "Maternal Thinking," in *Rethinking the Family*, ed. Barrie Thorne; and Christine E. Gudorf, "Parenting, Mutual Love and Sacrifice," in *Women's Consciousness, Women's Conscience: A Reader in Feminist Ethics*, ed. Barbara Andolsen (San Francisco: Harper and Row, 1987). Thomas M. Martin's *Christian Family Values* (New York: Paulist Press, 1984) presents a solid Protestant perspective on parenting and family life as does John H. Westerhoff's delightful *Bringing Up Children in the Christian Faith* (San Francisco: Harper and Row, 1980). Sofia Cavalletti's *The Religious Potential of the Child* (New York: Paulist Press, 1983) is a Montessori educator's contribution to our knowledge of children and religious education.

Chapter 8.

1. See for instance Mary Collins' 1987 Madeleva Lecture in Spirituality given at Notre Dame, published as *Women at Prayer* (New York: Paulist Press, 1987), which focuses upon writer Annie Dillard, poet Anne Sexton, and painter Meinrad Craighead.

Wreathed in Flesh and Warm

1. Robert Stephen Hawker, "Aisha Shekinah," in *Anthology of Catholic Poems,* ed. Leslie Chane (Darby, Penn.: Arden Library, 1978).

Chapter 9. Transfiguration

1. See, among others, Committee on Social Development and World Peace, *Violence in the Family* (Washington, D.C.: United States Catholic Conference, 1979), and David Cook and Anne Franz-Cook, "A Systematic Treatment Approach to Wife Battering," *Journal of Marital and Family Therapy,* 10, no. 1 (January 1984).

2. For a remarkable account of one woman's healing experience of forgiveness following the murder of her child, see Marietta Jeager, *The Lost Child* (Grand Rapids, Mich.: Zondervan, 1983).

3. See Dennis Linn, Matthew Linn, S.J., and Sheila Fabricant, *Healing the Eight Stages of Life* (Mahwah, N.J.: Paulist Press, 1988).

4. From "Let Us Walk in the Light," by Marty Haugen, copyright 1982 by Quiet Breeze Music, found in *Gather to Remember* (Chicago: GIA, 1982).

Chapter 10.

1. John Kavanaugh, S.J., writes with passion about these "idols" in *Following Christ in a Consumer Society* (Maryknoll, N.Y.: Orbis Books, 1981).

A Vowed Life

1. From *On Pilgrimage,* quoted in Dorothy Day, *Meditations,* pp. 58–59.

2. Ernest Boyer Jr.'s *A Way in the World: Family Life as Spiritual Discipline* (San Francisco: Harper and Row, 1984) is one of the best written books on family spirituality available.

3. Carol Orsborn, *Enough Is Enough: Exploding the Myth of Having It All* (New York: Putnam Pub., 1986) is an example of the literature on downward mobility.

4. See Jean Baker Miller, *Toward a New Psychology of Women* (Boston: Beacon Press, 1976).

5. The Christian churches in this country have issued a number of strong statements regarding the need for economic justice to be evaluated and practiced. They are *Social Principles* (Methodist, 1976), *Economic Justice: Stewardship of Human Creation and Community* (Lutheran, 1980), *Christian Faith and Justice* (Presbyterian, 1984), *Economic Justice for All* (Roman Catholic, 1986), *Christian Faith and Economic Rights* (United Church of Christ, 1986), and *Economic Justice and Christian Conscience* (Episcopalian, 1987).

LOOKING OUT

Chapter 11. Circles of Care

1. See especially Kathleen and James McGinnis, "The Social Mission of the Christian Family" in *Questions of Special Urgency*, ed. Judith A. Dwyer, S.S.J. (Washington, D.C.: Georgetown University Press, 1986), and Michael True, *Home Made Social Justice* (Mystic, Conn.: Twenty-Third Pubns., 1983). Both the Parenting for Peace and Justice Network (4144 Lindell Blvd., St. Louis, MO 63108) and the Christian Family Movement (P.O. Box 272, Ames, IA, 50010) provide extensive materials on Christian families and justice and peace issues.

2. The last chapter of Margaret R. Miles's book *Image as Insight: Visual Understanding in Western Christianity and Secular Culture* (Boston: Beacon Press, 1985) deals with this issue in contemporary terms.

Chapter 12. A Place of Springs

1. One booklet, *To Proclaim Peace: Religious Communities Speak Out on the Arms Race*, ed. John Donaghy (Nyack, N.Y.: Fellowship Pubns., 1983) contains statements about peace issued before 1983 by the American Baptist Church, American Lutheran Church, Armenian Church, Central Conference of American Rabbis, Disciples of Christ, Church of the Brethren, Mormons, Episcopal Church, Greek Orthodox Church, Lutheran Church in America, Mennonites, Presbyterian Church, Rabbinical Assembly, Reformed Church in America, Roman Catholic Church, Quakers, Southern Baptist Convention, Synagogue Council of America, and Unitarian Universalist Association. Since 1983 the Methodist, the Presbyterian, and the Roman Catholic communities have each issued major peace statements. See *In Defense of Creation: The Nuclear Crisis and a Just Peace* (1986) by the Bishops of the United Methodist Church, *Christian Obedience in a Nuclear Age* (1988) by the General Assembly of the Presbyterian church, and *The Challenge of Peace* (1983) by the National Conference of Catholic Bishops.

2. Refer to the McGinnis book *Parenting for Peace and Justice*, and Bob and Janet Aldridge, *Children and Nonviolence* (Pasadena, CA: Hope Publishing House, 1987). For a treatment of the faith experience of bringing children into the world in the nuclear age, see Denise Priestley, *Bringing Forth in Hope* (New York: Paulist Press, 1983).

Chapter 13. The *Is-ness* of Things

1. John M. Staudenmeier, *Technology's Storytellers: Reweaving the Human Fabric* (Cambridge, Mass.: MIT Press, 1985).

2. Charles Fenyvesi, "Where Our Roots Are," *Organic Gardening*, September 1987, pp. 102–3.